Some Necessary Questions
of the Play

Some Necessary Questions of the Play

A Stage-Centered Analysis of Shakespeare's *Hamlet*

Robert E. Wood

Lewisburg
Bucknell University Press
London and Toronto: Associated University Presses

Associated University Presses
440 Forsgate Drive
Cranbury, NJ 08512

Associated University Presses
25 Sicilian Avenue
London WC1A 2QH, England

Associated University Presses
P.O. Box 338, Port Credit
Mississauga, Ontario
Canada L5G 4L8

The paper used in this publication meets the requirements of the American National Standard for Permanence of Paper for Printed Library Materials 39.48–1984.

Library of Congress Cataloging-in-Publication Data

Wood, Robert E., 1944-
    Some necessary questions of the play : a stage-centered analysis of Shakespeare's Hamlet / Robert E. Wood.
        p. cm.
    Includes bibliographical references and index.
    ISBN Ø-8387-5290-X
    1. Shakespeare, William, 1564-1616. Hamlet. 2. Shakespeare, William, 1564-1616
--Dramatic production. 3. Theater--Production and direction. I. Title.
    PR2807.W59   1994
    822.3'3--dc20   94-11462
                                                                                          CIP

Printed in the United States of America

For Carolyn

Contents

Textual Note

Except where noted, I have used *The Riverside Shakespeare*, edited by G. Blakemore Evans (Boston: Houghton Mifflin, 1974) for all quotations from Shakespeare. I have, however, deleted the editorial brackets. Brackets in my text have their customary use.

Acknowledgments

I wish to thank Houghton Mifflin for permission to quote from *The Riverside Shakespeare*, edited by G. Blakemore Evans, and to Humanities University Press and Routledge for permission to quote from M. Merleau-Ponty, *Phenomenology of Perception*, translated by Colin Smith. A version of chapter 1 of my book first appeared in *South Atlantic Review*, and a version of chapter 2 first appeared in *Journal of Dramatic Theory and Criticism*. I would like to thank the editors of both journals for permission to publish as well as for the useful advice that the editorial process provided in the early stages of my project.

Early development of this work was assisted by a research grant from the Georgia Tech Foundation. Some of the initial ideas were born in an NEH seminar at Princeton with Daniel Seltzer. Of those administrators who supported the long process of bringing this book to completion, I particularly wish to thank Karl Murphy and Elizabeth Evans. I owe much to my colleagues, past and present, for creating an atmosphere conducive to intellectual work. I note, as particularly influential, Phil Auslander, Annibel Jenkins, Ken Knoespel, Paul Privateer, Jay Telotte, and Cynthia Thomizer.

Thanks are due to the editors and readers of Bucknell University Press for their interest in this work and to the editors of Associated University Presses for their assistance in sparing the reader more than a few oversights and infelicities.

My greatest debt is to my family for their support and encouragement. My children — Kathy, Michael, and Elizabeth — have been an antidote to melancholy sufficient even for the Dane. My wife, Carolyn, has and deserves my greatest thanks.

Introduction

Stage-centered criticism of drama is no longer new, and it is probably no longer necessary to explain that this criticism is no antagonist of the criticism of the text. Among other possibilities, it may be a criticism of the text weighted to acknowledge the realities of theatrical perception: the experience of space and time; the nature of spoken language; the mutual presence of actors and audience; the conventions and expectations that facilitate dramatic compression. The greatest contribution of stage-centered criticism may be common sense, conceived in an almost classical way as the synthesis of the sensory impressions which inform us. What may be achieved is an interpretation which balances the contributions of all the resources of the theater on which the play depends.

Shakespeare studies have been perhaps the greatest beneficiary of stage-centered criticism not only because enormous resources of energy are inevitably invested in any new approach to Shakespeare's work, but also for intrinsic reasons. Historically, Shakespeare's career took place during a period of intense theatrical experimentation, and he responded to almost every aspect of that experimentation. Moreover, each major play in the canon has been subjected to the entire spectrum of theatrical innovations and ideological stances that have followed the Renaissance, variously appropriating, renewing, or restoring the plays. Both historical inquiry and ongoing experimentation return the text to the stage. What we have thought has been put into practice, and our practice has in turn been analyzed. The volume of theatrical activity has allowed widely divergent alternatives to be explored. We have built stages like the Globe and, sometimes on those very stages, performed versions of Shakespeare steeped in Freud or Sartre. On the whole, a return to the origins of Shakespearean production has been fruitful. In the bareness of the Elizabethan stage, we have found not only the power of Shakespeare's poetry, which has never been in question, but the power to evoke with spoken words an experience in space and time.[1] At some point experiments with Shakespeare's plays become the renegotiation of cultural myths. While my study does not focus on such experiments, I am interested in those properties of the play *Hamlet* which have made it a territory for cultural renegotiation.

To examine *Hamlet* as a text conceived not only for the theater but within it is not, then, a new task. For all our use of Shakespeare as Great Book or cultural icon, or even as the raw material for a scholarly industry, our interest in the "wooden O" has never really abated. Yet for this very reason, such an examination of *Hamlet* is always a new task as we continually renew our perspectives not only on the play but on the theater itself. In the twentieth century, the theater has been moved radically to redefine itself. Cinema, radio, and television compete not only for the ears and eyes of the populace but also for the talents of the creative artists who constitute a theater: the writers, actors, directors, designers, musicians, and technicians. The theater has survived, has continued to attract both audiences and creative talent, because we have come to appreciate its unique use of space, time, and presence.

The renewal of the theater has been largely a project of clarification. Alternative modes of dramatization like the cinema have provided not only the stimulus of competition but the contrast that has helped to define the intrinsic attributes of the theater. And as we become more explicit about what is happening in the theater, we find new things to say about what the dramatic text does there. In discussing the text in the theater, however, we must distinguish between what the text does in the theater and what happens when it is performed. The performance text, that is, the performance considered as a text, is the product both of creative efforts beyond those of the original author and of the specific accidents of the real-time enactment. In the contemporary theater, in fact, struggles between performing groups and authors for control of the performance text have occurred in locations ranging from the public forum to the public courts.

A performance is both a creative act and an act of interpretation. The success of the creative act may well be independent of the validity of the interpretive act. Thus in any actual performance we see the impact of the dramatic text on the stage as in a glass darkly. Nonetheless, there are useful ways of contemplating our experience of the text in the theater.

Marvin Rosenberg's studies of Shakespeare's major tragedies categorize the range of performances they have generated. This very variability can be seen as an intrinsic property of the plays. J. L. Styan's *The Shakespearean Revolution* examines the impact of our changing understanding of the theatrical contract that governs relations among audience, performers, and text. Michael Goldman's approaches to drama keep us in touch with the relation of the dramatic text to theatrical theory and to the abstract potential of theatrical performance.[2]

In this very fluid realm of discourse, I launch my study of *Hamlet*. I must confess that at some point early in my contemplation of the play I entertained the illusion of viewing this study as a paradigm of how to approach the dramatic text in the theatrical context. The illusion had a certain naive plausibility. The image of the dark-costumed Elizabethan is at once a sign for "Hamlet" and for "actor." The play is both a classic and a stirring contemporary drama. It is variable and yet always identifiable. Its protagonist theorizes about self and about the theater. Yet in practice, the very process of exploring how *Hamlet* is situated in the theater reveals that every choice that distinguishes the play suggests viable alternatives to those choices, other ways of dramatizing. Moreover, the play is continually demolishing our frameworks, funneling through the protagonist's consciousness our consideration of space and time, of language, of genre, and even of the body.

It is not my purpose to reject what has been thought and written about *Hamlet* for four hundred years, nor is it my intention to reiterate it. In recent years our disputations about interpretations have been displaced by a debate of discourses that seeks to determine what kind of conversations we should be having about literature. Shakespeare's plays are the ground of a number of such controversies. We are already in controversy simply in calling the plays literature, given that they are designed for theatrical presentation. Yet the rich language of the Shakespearean text continues to reward literary approaches. When we turn to theatrical theory, we encounter a battleground of sorts if we attempt to explore the ground between the dramatic text and the performance text. Nor is the cultural context of the plays a given. Arguments continue not only over the relationship of a play like *Hamlet* to its originating culture but over the role of such a cultural counter in contemporary struggles over cultural hegemony.

In my approach to *Hamlet* then, whatever explicit conflicts with alternative critical stances may appear, my primary contention remains that it is valuable to talk about this text in this way. By invoking semiotics, semiology, and phenomenology, I hope to be more than merely fashionable. It is essential to my project to talk about how the theater addresses us without words, but at the same time it would be absurd to lessen the weight of words in such a play as *Hamlet*. The phenomenology of perception, as formulated by Merleau-Ponty, by positing the wholeness of perception, allows the reintegration of what analytic methods naturally divide.[3] By periodically insisting on the integrating power of perception, I hope for a more "arthroscopic" analysis that allows us not to lose sight of our behavior as an audience, our constant process of making sense of what evolves before us.

As an audience, we are moved not only by verbal devices but by such diverse attributes of the theater as space, time, and bodily presence. In *Hamlet* these attributes are used in a unified way to direct our perception; most of the time this means to align our perception with that of the protagonist. This perceptual alignment is distinct from an alignment of values, such as we might have with Prince Hal if we accept the mythic pattern of the Henriad. It also differs from the simple empathy we might have with any tragic figure — Macbeth, for example — with whom we empathize, though his vision of the world is never our own.

Because space, time, and bodily presence act on our perceptions in a way consistent with how the play's words act on us, the reading of *Hamlet* as a book rather than as a script has not been categorically misleading. Most of the play's gestures in space and time are verbal. Hamlet is, of course, a highly articulate character in a poetic drama, a genre in which any character is normally articulate. In reading the book, however, at least in reading it as critics, we tend to accept the hermeneutic assumption that the text is always present in its totality. But the readers who move through the book are not the same as the audience that is moved through the play. For an audience, the very process of perception is altered as the play proceeds. We feel a sense of collective passage. The mutual presence of actors and audience moves us to harmony. We have also invested the theater space with meaning as we attend to the dramatic narrative. Because the process of perception normally varies as a play proceeds, it is inherently subject to manipulation. As I have suggested, *Hamlet* makes particular use of this variability, so much so that while we are baffled in our attempts to explain what changes materially between Acts I and V, we have no difficulty in understanding that Hamlet perceives things differently.

This line of inquiry suggests an abstract theatrical context for *Hamlet*. Why then this abstract context rather than one specifically Elizabethan, to reflect the play's originating culture, or specifically contemporary, to reflect our own? I believe this abstraction is natural to the play. In general, I subscribe to Stephen Greenblatt's contention that the totalizing impulse of Tudor-Stuart culture was not absolute.[4] In particular, I think we are justified in observing that Shakespeare was afforded (and took) liberties with the representation of alien cultures that would not have been permitted in the English history plays. This is not to say that he undertook a systematic program of subverting his society's values, but rather that he could allow more interesting questions to be raised because he was not compelled to reproduce the Tudor-Stuart worldview by the play's end. The current relevance of *Hamlet* emanates from that movement away from Tudor cultural resolutions, a movement which never replaces them with alternative resolutions. The modernity of the play consists both in our general tendency to value that which continues to interrogate and in our ability to shape the play's interrogation in performance. Performance periodically generates a "Hamlet for our time" — that is, one whose questioning of established values reflects the contemporary style for such questioning, be it Freudian, existentialist, Marxist, or that of one of their postmodern heirs.

My study begins with an examination of *Hamlet*'s use of real space and time as elements of a narration which is in part about a protagonist's perception of space and time. Although the examination resists the reduction of time to a spatial analogy, it shows that corresponding distortions in the protagonist's perception of space and time accompany his disillusionment with cultural values. In its restriction of the customary scope of the Elizabethan stage representation of space, the play reflects Hamlet's perception of space as restricted. Our sense that the tempo of *Hamlet* is somehow incompatible with the concept of hesitation receives some satisfaction in a phenomenological view of the protagonist's perception of time. Hamlet's refusal to take up the past and project the future creates in him a sense of stasis even in the midst of his most frenetic activity. As an audience, we are led to share his intense contemplation of the passing time in which the drama itself is grounded.

The next phase of my study examines two aspects of Hamlet's

language, wit, and soliloquy. Though not inherently at odds, wit and soliloquy become mutually exclusive alternatives in the protagonist's interrogation of language. Hamlet's wit assaults language at the level of the word. His soliloquies attack language less directly: they exhaust its modes of discourse without moving toward resolution. Wit disrupts dialogue by denying its logic. Soliloquy displaces dialogue, replacing it with monologue. In combination, wit and soliloquy disrupt the normal language of drama. Act V marks the end of this dislocation and, significantly, the end of Hamlet's distorted perception of space and time as well.

The third and final phase of my study examines expectations we bring to the theater: our focus on the body as the locus of our attention, and our understanding of the generic framework which orders our experience. Far from being a neutral element in dramatic composition, the body is already imbued with expectation both in the culture at large and in the theatrical context. A phenomenology of perception links our observations about the body with what has been said about space, time, and language. The body is viewed as the source of gesture, a concept which includes language as gesture. Gesture is viewed as a correspondence of the actor's body to the body of each perceiver. Thus the audience traces the actor bodily and shares, at some level, the actor's perceptual framework. This general process is of fundamental importance in *Hamlet*, where the protagonist's perceptual shift is essential to our experience of the play.

The genre of a play is important to the theatrical event as a set of expectations that make possible our common experience. I examine issues of genre in *Hamlet* to determine if these generic expectations lead us toward the experience of Hamlet's perceptual shifts or direct us from them. What we find in the play is an orderly series of violations of the generic expectations of revenge tragedy which opens up the rather narrow range of problems germane to that genre into the fuller scope of tragedy proper. Within this larger scope, the complex problems of Hamlet's subjectivity invite our attention. Because *Hamlet* problematizes genre, we become aware of the problems inherent in dramatizing saga, problems generated by infusing mythic narrative with consciousness. Such considerations are of vital interest to any theater which attempts to integrate ritual with psychological realism. The ambivalence of the generic framework of *Hamlet* makes its questions no longer conventions, and thus makes its generalized challenge to the institutions of social order unconventional. To construct this analysis of genre is, in part, to formalize for the scholar what has long been theatrical practice, legitimizing the pleasures of the legitimate theater. At the same time, the theatrical practitioner is invited to view the scholarly tradition as an ongoing expansion of possibilities rather than as a corrective to theatrical heresies.

This analysis does not, for the most part, dictate the approach to particular scenes or lines of the play, but it does raise for the actor or director a set of questions quite different from those which would be raised by a strictly literary analysis of the play. I contend that because the play depends upon the protagonist's shifting and interconnected perceptions of space, time, language, and the body, every production decision has an exaggerated and often unexpected impact on the dynamics of the play. Every set design becomes an essay on *Hamlet*.

I recall being distracted by a monumental statue, presumably of Claudius, utilized in the 1989 National Theatre (London) production of *Hamlet* with Daniel Day-Lewis. Overshadowed by the statue, Hamlet's body was inevitably small and his subjective attitude toward his own body and the space it inhabited diminished in importance. Though few scholars would quarrel with the idea underlying this massive presence of the King, such a design communicates about the body rather than through the body and disrupts our psychological alignment with Hamlet's subjectivity.

On the other hand, controversial interpretive issues of considerable magnitude may have comparatively minor effects on the dynamics of performance. The Freudian interpretation of *Hamlet*, which views Hamlet as struggling against a reversion to the Oedipal crisis, has enjoyed a long run in the theater despite the objections of most scholars and the incredulity of generations of undergraduates. I suggest that this interpretation persists as a performance concept because it does not disturb what I call the phenomenological argument of the play. The Freudian reading suggests why Hamlet perceives the world as he does, but *it* does not change that perception. On the stage, the seemingly requisite unfilial kiss and the bed in Gertrude's closet have little impact on the rhythms of the play.

If, however, a production experiments with Hamlet's symptoms rather than the underlying causes of his instability, the performance is more radically altered. The 1989 Royal Shakespeare Company (Stratford) production of *Hamlet* with Mark Rylance presented a truly debilitated protagonist, credibly resembling a neglected mental patient. Such a Hamlet was in no position to dominate the space with the power of his wit. Indeed, in the resulting power vacuum, Rosencrantz and Guildenstern became schoolyard bullies rather than anonymous collaborators with the King. In compensation, the approach left Rylance in a good position to mark Hamlet's transition to strength in Act V, and to convey the search for strength in soliloquy.

I am not suggesting that we replace a stultifying orthodoxy of ideas with a stultifying orthodoxy of structure. Production decisions against the grain of the play may result in stunning successes, but such successes will tend to be admired rather than imitated. To my mind, Rylance's Hamlet achieved a success of this nature due in part to the audience's awareness that the production boldly departed from the traditional line. There is a fascination in losing Hamlet and finding him again that sustains our interest in experimental approaches to the play.

Film versions of *Hamlet* present us with a completely different relationship of audience to text than that which is explored in this study. Nevertheless, film Hamlets, "the cousins," if you will, of their stage counterparts, continue to affect our collective understanding of Hamlet. Because films reach a mass audience and are accessible to succeeding generations, they constitute a common experience as no single theatrical performance can. As common experience, film versions of *Hamlet* will continue to be examined as visualizations of the play *Hamlet,* and it is in this vein that I offer a few suggestions.

The approach to *Hamlet* proposed in this study cannot be used to evaluate the merits of a film as film, but it can be used to examine the effects of cinematic choices on what I call the phenomenological argument of the play. For example, among the inevitable choices made in a film version of *Hamlet* is how to transpose stage space to film space. The play resists the customary response of opening up stage space. Olivier (1948) conveyed Hamlet's sense of confinement through slow tracking shots in a labyrinthine Elsinore. Zeffirelli (1990), on the other hand, placed Hamlet on horseback in the full light of day, subverting that sense of confinement.

Some of the concerns of my approach might address film as a medium rather than a specific production. For example, film has no inherent problem with wit yet seems inevitably to struggle with soliloquy, usually by attempting to justify or obliterate the stage convention. My study argues that the balance between soliloquy and wit is fundamental to the dynamics of *Hamlet*, and thus I would maintain that the disruption of this balance has serious consequences, among them the muting of the whole issue of Hamlet's hesitation. My feeling is that the convention of soliloquy is better accepted than evaded. A remarkable framework for soliloquy usually creates an unremarkable soliloquy. The treatment of time in film follows different conventions from those in the theater, but it is possible to trace Hamlet's perception of time in either medium. What is important is keeping our perception of time attuned to Hamlet's subjectivity, rather than objectifying the play's references to time as if they could be considered independently.

The considerations of this study represent if not a unified theory of theatrical expression at least a series of "necessary questions" about the structural considerations that make possible the multiplicity of contemporary approaches to *Hamlet*. Ultimately, the play's logical coherence is to be found in the theater viewed not only as the moving moment of performance but also as all the thought that enables performance and all that emanates from it. If I claimed one virtue for my approach, it would not be that it dominates a debate but that it refuses to disengage itself from other approaches. I think of this book as having something to say about our common experience of the play.

Some Necessary Questions
of the Play

Part I
Space and Time

1

Space and Scrutiny in *Hamlet*

The space in which drama takes place is inherently ambiguous. In its origins, the stage is an extended altar, a real place in which human actions can invoke the presence of the sacred or focus the perception of a god on the intentions of the human beings gathered there. At the point when people act to show consequences rather than create consequences, the place in which they act is used as a stage rather than an altar. The distinction is not always easily made, particularly as drama seems universally to develop through religious festivals; but the development of significant bodies of drama has not occurred without this distinction.

A stage is, then, before anything, a space in which virtual actions can take place. Characters, who are constituted by these virtual actions, are placed in proximity to each other, a proximity within which their conflicting objectives will force them to operate on each other either verbally or physically.[1] If in addition the stage represents some geographic locality, it does so because the drama concerns the consequences of actions in that particular locality. But we have often seen successful productions of classic drama in new settings which preserve the pattern of actions that constitute the play's essential identity. Regardless of how many places are associated with the stage in the course of a performance, it remains principally the space where actions are represented for an audience. At any given moment, any place other than that of the stage action, no matter how thoroughly established by the text of the play as a whole, is perceived by the audience as having a contingent existence that must be related to the visible stage.[2] In general a drama permits an audience to consider characters as having three kinds of relationship to the visible

27

stage: presence, extreme distance, and intermediate distance (or momentary absence). The distinction between intermediate and extreme distance is that the character in extreme distance is presumed to be inaccessible to the action of the stage scene, whereas a character in intermediate distance may be as relevant to the immediate expectations of the audience as the characters onstage. In classical Greek drama, for example, the most conspicuous place of intermediate presence is the skene, in most cases representing a palace. Characters known to be within the skene in circumstances expected to produce violence are part of the perception of the audience. Examples are easily found. Vowing vengeance, Euripides' Medea enters a palace with her children. Foreseeing violence, Aeschylus's Cassandra enters a palace where she will be killed. The chorus (and audience) await the result of what they perceive as a dangerous encounter within. Extreme distance in Greek drama is a place from which someone may arrive prepared to alter circumstances which are well-defined preceding his arrival. In the *Oresteia,* the successive arrivals of Agamemnon, Orestes, and the Eumenides produce scenes of new conflict. The arrival in *Oedipus Rex* of a series of messengers provides information that alters the relationship of the principal characters to each other and to themselves.

Shakespeare's stage is more complex because the same three relationships to the stage space remain, but that space itself may take on several identities. The characteristic Elizabethan double-plot drama, which establishes two geographic places, focuses on actions at both ends of extreme distance — Egypt and Rome; the Boar's Head Tavern and the throne of England. Physical distances are relatively unimportant. They exist to establish partitions. Cleopatra cannot enter a scene in Rome; King Henry cannot enter the Boar's Head Tavern. In their absence from scenes in these places, they are always at extreme distance, never intermediate. The focal point remains the space in which action takes place at a given moment.

When stage space represents a geographic place, the concept of territory becomes important. In ritual, in the presence of the gods, the concept of territory has no validity. In a representation of struggle between gods and men it has no relevance. In a struggle between human beings, territory becomes primary. We may ask: to whom does the space in which conflict occurs belong? Whose place is it? Who is a stranger to the place? The concept of place, like that of space, is related to character, but rather than being merely the proximity of characters, place is their proximity in a space controlled by one of the characters. The feasibility of changing setting in a drama and preserving the conflict essentially intact is a result of the priority of the relation of the characters to the place over the relationship of the place to the world in which it has geographic and historical coordinates.

Place becomes a significant setting to the degree to which the historical and geographic coordinates are significant to the action. Chekhov's *Cherry Orchard* is centrally concerned with the relationship of people to the land. The presence of the orchard just offstage is as significant to the action onstage as are the characters within the skene in Greek drama. Setting determines that Shakespeare's English history plays are plays about history, whereas the Roman plays, though based on history, are plays about politics. The difference lies in the relative priority of assertions of obligation to the land. In both Chekhov's plays and the English history plays, characters are judged through the effect of their actions on their relationship to the land. Setting in drama becomes still more significant in naturalistic (as distinct from realistic) drama, where environment is represented as a significant determinant of action, as in most of the work by Arthur Miller. The use of stage space may in fact come full circle when urban landlessness creates a setting equivalent to abstract space, with the difference being that the absence of connection to the land is perceived as loss. Ionesco's barren cityscapes convey this effect.

Considered within this framework, the significance of the substantial "unity of place" in *Hamlet* is that the characters in conflict with each other (until Hamlet's sea voyage) have access to each other at all times. In any scene, the missing characters are located at an intermediate distance from the stage — their presence is imminent. The space of the action is a territory; that is, Claudius is in possession of a place that ought to be Hamlet's, and they are engaged in a struggle for that place. Because Claudius's crime consisted of taking Hamlet Senior's place, in all the ramifications of the term, even the obligation of revenge has a territorial basis. But despite the existence of a real Elsinore, Shakespeare's Elsinore has none of the characteristics of significant setting — it has no historical or geographic roots of importance to the action. The place that Hamlet and Claudius fight for is almost as arbitrary as the battlefield where Fortinbras chooses to stake his honor. The suggestion of a Denmark outside Elsinore is extremely limited. To some extent a barely defined

populace limits the capacity for tyranny of the King and perhaps influences the behavior of Hamlet as well. But the influence of this populace
is completely internalized. (Even the small popular uprising that Laertes
leads late in the play is represented by his solitary presence and the sound
of voices from offstage.)

The modernity of the play derives in part from our perception that the
use of space in the play is a restriction of the uses of space normal to
Elizabethan theater. Violent passions dominate *Hamlet*, but straightfor-
wardly violent actions are excluded from the stage. Fortinbras's wars, the
fight at sea, and Ophelia's drowning are distanced through narration,
whereas onstage violence is consistently indirect. All four deaths in Act
V are caused by poison, and the heroic potential of the duel is dissipated.
In addition, the play erects barriers to envisioning alternatives to
Elsinore. In *Macbeth*, England is a haven where norms of value can be
reestablished at a distance from the corrupt court of the usurper. In
Hamlet, England reinforces the corruption of the Danish court by providing executions as a diplomatic courtesy. The Elizabethan audience is thus
in some sense denied its avenue of retreat. Even scenes outside Elsinore
proper intensify the sense of confinement. The plain in Denmark where
Hamlet encounters Fortinbras's army allows a contemplation of the
confined space within which Fortinbras will fight. The graveyard, not
inaccessible to the court, provides no distance from Elsinore. Ophelia's
grave represents the ultimate confinement, and, in Hamlet's struggle with
Laertes, the smallest field of conflict. *Hamlet* creates a sense of loss
because of alternatives not taken; "unity of place" in *Hamlet* is not a
classical unity but a palpable confinement.[3]

An important spatial consideration in *Hamlet* is the proximity of characters to each other. The most pervasive activity in the play is scrutiny.
Characters in *Hamlet* eavesdrop on each other; in dialogue, they observe
each other's behavior for the purpose of discerning underlying intention;
they create scenarios to isolate reactions to some particular stimuli. Their
precise proximity to each other is of the essence of the subtle judgments
that order their conflicts. Yet the first bloodletting within the play, the
death of Polonius, results from the crudest of mistakes, a mistake in
identity in a play where characters aspire to read each other's thoughts.

The only place in the play exempt from the antagonistic scrutiny that
characterizes human relations is the castle platform exterior to Elsinore.
Although the scenes on the battlements in Act I are cold, dark, and

menaced by the supernatural, the place is not frequented by betrayers. The explicit dangers of the wall — the elements of nature, the potential for armed conflict, the threat from the spirit world — partition the area from the miasma within the castle. The atmosphere of the wall is martial: armed men encounter an armed ghost on what might be the eve of war. The risk Hamlet undertakes in pursuing the ghost is enhanced by the prospect of his being lured to a fall. The extraordinary mobility of the ghost, whom Hamlet must pursue through shifts of locale on and under the stage, lends to the scene a physical openness that contrasts sharply with the action that subsequently takes place within the castle. A partition seems to be erected both by the nature of the movement that takes place during the scenes on the battlements and by the moral character of the persons who are there.

Hamlet's father, the focal point of the battlement scenes, is an honest ghost whose desire for revenge is not unbounded: he would leave the punishment of Gertrude to heaven. Of the natural characters who appear on the battlements, only Horatio encounters Hamlet again. Horatio is both completely trusted and trustworthy. The soldiers whom we never again encounter after Act I can be assumed to have kept their word — a betrayal would have had some palpable consequence. More pointedly, Hamlet assumes not only that they will be bound by their oath not to reveal what they have seen, but that they can be trusted not to reveal that his antic disposition is "put on." Further, they can be trusted not to suggest, by hinting that they know more than they can say, directions for scrutiny. In clear contrast, every resident of Elsinore not present on the battlements subsequently participates in betraying or deceiving Hamlet.

Within Elsinore, the uses of proximity are those more naturally associated with comedy than with tragedy. The scene from II.i to IV.iii, confined to the castle, consists almost entirely of scenarios devised to test the emotional reactions of antagonists. Polonius, Ophelia, and Rosencrantz and Guildenstern are sent to converse with Hamlet in order to learn his purposes. Ophelia, the most innocent of these pawns, is seconded by the King's party overhearing her and Hamlet from behind a curtain. Hamlet in counterplot contrives the Mousetrap play at which he observes Claudius. And he confronts Gertrude in order to stir her conscience by threatening her life. The latter device is overheard, with disastrous consequence, by the eavesdropping Polonius. Elsinore, in short, has more hidden observers than a French farce.

So much is evident. Only slightly less so is the intensity with which scrutiny excludes all else from consideration. The ambassadors returning from Norway are quickly dealt with, and only at Polonius's request are they entertained before the King hears news of Hamlet. The only event between the ghost's visit and Hamlet's exile that is not ultimately concerned with scrutinizing either Hamlet or Claudius is that in which Polonius instructs Reynaldo on how to obtain information about Laertes at a distance. The style of interrogation that Polonius advocates reflects his approach to inquiry about Hamlet.[4] Reynaldo is to speak of Laertes' supposed youthful indiscretions in an attempt to encourage his companions in Paris to contribute information of their own.

> See you now,
> Your bait of falsehood take this carp of truth,
> And thus do we of wisdom and of reach,
> With windlasses and with assays of bias,
> By indirections find directions out.

                                                    (II.i.59–65)

The plan seems feasible and, within the restrictions Polonius imposes on Reynaldo, harmless enough. But in the closed world of Elsinore, each such inquiry generates misinformation and contaminates the inquirer. Because words no longer represent truth, knowledge cannot be shared or accumulated. The individual must examine the world for himself by experiencing it. Even the major soliloquies of this section give priority to experience. Hamlet's "O what a rogue" and "To be or not to be" explore the borders of the knowable and conclude that knowing guilt or death will depend on an observer's "being there."

Confronting a spirit, Hamlet is denied his most reliable sense. The ghost cannot be known by seeing because his shape may be assumed. Words, no more reliable than the speaker, will prove nothing in Elsinore.[5]

> The spirit that I have seen
> May be a dev'l, and the dev'l hath power
> T'assume a pleasing shape, yea, and perhaps,
> Out of my weakness and my melancholy,
> As he is very potent with such spirits,
> Abuses me to damn me. I'll have grounds

> More relative than this — the play's the thing
> Wherein I'll catch the conscience of the King.
>
> (II.ii.598–605)

The ghost cannot be scrutinized. His words can be verified only by examining their consequences in the physical world. The King, however, can be known by the sight of his reaction to the play. He can be known through experiment, not by the actions he chooses (he can smile and be a villain), but by his involuntary reaction to a contrived situation. Paradox-ically, to learn the truth, Hamlet relies upon the players' powers of simulation, the "dream of passion." Faced with unreliable seeming and unreliable speaking, Hamlet resolves to penetrate the seeming, a logical choice because the degree of mediation involved in words is irreducible. Philosophical scrutiny is discounted in favor of that scrutiny which involves careful observation.

Given the emphasis on experience in *Hamlet* and the consequent reliance on the senses, a peculiarity in the soliloquy "To be or not to be" becomes less puzzling. Despite the appearance of the ghost, the world beyond death is "The undiscover'd country, from whose bourn / No traveler returns." Hamlet Senior does not, in fact, return from death to life. His form remains impalpable and, though his word ultimately proves reliable, he is "forbid / To tell the secrets of [his] prison house." Not knowing what death is, but constrained by the existence of the ghost to regard it as an experience rather than a termination, Hamlet plausibly fears "what dreams may come." Moreover, his later hesitation to kill the King at prayer must reflect in part the view that to kill the King is to translate his problem, not to solve it. The felicity of death that Hamlet alludes to in Act V is apprehended by faith. Experience tells him not that life is eternal but that it is interminable. For all the confinement of Elsinore, Hamlet's greatest problem lies at an infinite distance from him, that is, beyond the senses.[6]

Acts of physical observation in *Hamlet* are characterized by the limi-tations of the senses. Barriers to sight are the simplest limitations. The greatest mistaking of the play occurs when Hamlet and Polonius are separated by an arras in Gertrude's closet. Polonius mistakes Hamlet's threats for an attempted murder. Hamlet mistakes Polonius for the King — the voice is not sufficient for recognition. The King's earliest stratagem is more typical of the problems of observation. When Ophelia is loosed to Hamlet, Claudius and Polonius find a vantage point where they can see unseen. That their vantage point is traditionally from behind a curtain is unnecessary to make the point. The act of espial is a limited form of observation. Polonius is duped, Claudius unconvinced. The event is perceived differently by the two observers. Ophelia offers yet a third perspective: her direct encounter with Hamlet allows her to experience his emotional ambivalence toward her. None of the three is both close enough to appraise the situation and disengaged enough to evaluate it.

The Mousetrap play becomes the paradigm of observation. At the performance, Hamlet's vantage point is unrestricted. His observation is confirmed by that of Horatio, a wiser second than Polonius. He is in control of the sequence of events: knowing the plot of the play and the location of the interpolated speech, he knows at which point of the play to expect a psychological crisis in Claudius. Moreover, he informs Horatio of this critical point and agrees to compare judgments with him afterwards. In addition, he posits the possibility that the King will not react, in which case he is, or at least claims to be, willing to dismiss his suspicions. Although the objectivity of the experiment is disturbed in practice by Hamlet's emotional reaction, the endeavor is unique. No avenger in Elizabethan drama performs a comparable experiment to determine the guilt of his victim.[7]

The Mousetrap experiment is surrounded by illustrations of the problems of observation under uncontrolled circumstances. The espial, which we have briefly discussed, of the conversation between Ophelia and Hamlet is unscripted — Ophelia is not entirely an instrument. Thus Claudius and Polonius observe too much and not enough. Hamlet's attitude toward the King (and Queen) is complicated by his relation to Ophelia. Polonius and Claudius each perceive one dimension of his behavior, but because they cannot agree about what they are looking for, they cannot reconcile what they have seen. Polonius proposes a second observation — a conference with the Queen *after* the players perform. Polonius's strategy is to arrange a series of confrontations, one of which he hopes will result in an articulate confession, that is Hamlet's objective analysis of his own behavior. The approach parallels that which he uses to investigate his own son. But because Hamlet is not naive, nor Claudius paternal, his gentle chicanery serves only to widen the scope of their deadly conflict.

A more promising approach is the use of Rosencrantz and Guildenstern as instruments to examine Hamlet. That they are strangers to the events that precede Hamlet's mad behavior reduces the complexity of his reaction to them, but they are enjoined "to gather / So much as from occasion [they] may glean." The process of observation remains uncontrolled. They are in fact at a disadvantage in encountering Hamlet, who easily ascertains that they were sent for as observers. In the aftermath of the Mousetrap, he mocks their attempts to manipulate him, to play on him as on a pipe. In fact, they "have not the skill" for either instrument. The ultimate ineffectiveness of this approach to Hamlet is aptly summarized by Rosencrantz:

> He does confess he feels himself distracted,
> But from what cause 'a will by no means speak.
>
> (III.i.5–6)

Tom Stoppard's *Rosencrantz and Guildenstern Are Dead* is a monument to their confusion. They know neither what they are looking for nor what is anomalous enough to be reported to a more informed analyst.

The problem of observing is compounded when the senses are deprived of access to what is being observed. Polonius bases his theory of the cause of Hamlet's madness on a twice-removed observation — Ophelia's narrative account of the dumb show that Hamlet performs in her chamber. Hamlet's miming allows him to display emotion without articulating its cause, an eventuality unlikely in dialogue and in fact possible only by the deliberate refusal to respond to an inevitable question. Nor is his visit mere display. Her narration describes Hamlet making "such perusal of [her] face / As 'a would draw it." She observes that he observes her, but they apparently remain enigmatic to each other.

It is far from surprising that Claudius does not react immediately to the dumb show that precedes the Mousetrap play. Only the most careful and sustained observation is presented in this section of *Hamlet* as being capable of yielding information. It is consistent with other acts of scrutiny in the play that the stylized visual representation of the murder can at most begin to attract the attention of the King. When the dialogue of the Mousetrap commences, he is prepared to observe and is thus susceptible to the psychological assault that ensues. The play is of course designed not merely to allow him to notice that it echoes his crime but to force an emotional reaction.[8]

Of all the acts of observation in the interior of Elsinore only one is not a result of contrivance. Hamlet discovers Claudius at prayer, but because he sees the King kneeling without being able to hear him and determine the ineffectiveness of the act of prayer, Hamlet misjudges the moment. The obstacles to prayer for Claudius and the failure of his prayer are articulated only at moments when Hamlet is offstage. But more significant than the mechanics of Hamlet's inability to hear Claudius's words is another barrier: prayer is essentially an interior act which is equivalent neither to its words nor to its gestures.

The most unusual scene of observation takes place in the Queen's closet. The perils of veiled observation are made manifest when Polonius is stabbed as he listens from behind the curtain. But far more interesting is Hamlet's argument to convince his mother of her folly. Initially, he reproaches her for her lust by asking her to compare two pictures, "The counterfeit presentment of two brothers." Under his reproaches and in contemplation of the two portraits she acknowledges her sins: "Thou turn'st my eyes into my very soul, / And there I see such black and grained spots / As will not leave their tinct." Yet thus far in the scene the mirror he holds is metaphoric, the pictures at best subjective images, and the insight intellectual. This kind of vision is not dependent on physical proximity but on the mind's eye. But the entry of the ghost returns us to a focus on the senses.

Hamlet sees the ghost and his mother does not. She is the only one in the play who does not see the ghost when he is present. His objective reality has been carefully established through multiple observers earlier in the play. They all see the ghost at the same time and see the same thing: a silver-bearded man in armor. In Gertrude's closet, his existence is in question. The motive of his appearance seems also to have evolved. Although the ghost reminds Hamlet of his duty to revenge, his greater concern seems to be for Gertrude.[9]

> But look, amazement on thy mother sits,
> O, step between her and her fighting soul.
> Conceit in weakest bodies strongest works,
> Speak to her, Hamlet.

(III.iv.112–15)

In simplistic terms, a man is talking to a ghost who warns him that his
mother, being weak in body (in the context of her relation to Claudius,
this would mean susceptible to the influence of her senses), is vulnerable
to her imagination. She in turn has observed Hamlet minutely.

> Alas, how is't with you,
> That you do bend your eye on vacancy,
> And with th' incorporal air do hold discourse?
> Forth at your eyes your spirits wildly peep,
> And as the sleeping soldiers in th' alarm
> Your bedded hair, like life in excrements,
> Start up and stand an end.
>
> (III.iv.116–22)

The issue that is pursued in the dialogue between Hamlet and Gertrude
is that he sees and hears something which occupies a specific space on
the stage that she perceives as vacant air. "Do you see nothing there?" he
asks. "Nor did you nothing hear?" He is careful in his verb tenses to
specify that the sight remains though the sound has ceased. In the face of
their completely divergent perception of reality (as distinct from
conception of reality) he must reestablish her belief in his sanity. He cites
the regularity of his pulse and his ability to remember and reiterate what
he has said.

> My pulse as yours doth temperately keep time,
> And makes as healthful music. It is not madness
> That I have utt'red. Bring me to the test,
> And I the matter will reword, which madness
> Would gambol from.
>
> (III.iv.140–44)

Her observations about his physical reactions are countered by his
interpretations of them. He cannot make her see the ghost, but he can
describe what he has seen and repeat what he has said precisely and in
response to direct questions.

The sensory bias to seeing and hearing on the stage is in part an
extension of our natural bias to these senses. We are used to quantifying
what we see and hear and to perceiving our universe in the measures
these senses suggest. More pertinent to the concerns of the stage, sight

and hearing are "public senses": an audience can share sights and sounds
with the characters in a drama as it cannot share touch, taste, and smell. [10]
Moreover, an audience can judge sight and sound independently of the
characters. We judge for ourselves the shrillness of a voice, the length of
a nose, the appearance of a king. We must accept the smell of a flower,
the warmth of an evening, and the delicacy of the wine. We need only
turn to Proust to see the greater democracy of the senses in a purely verbal medium where no sensory perception has priority — the taste of the
madeleine, the sound of a musical phrase, and the sight of church spires
are equally accessible (or, if we prefer, equally mysterious). But the stage
singles out sight and sound; the players, had they Hamlet's motive,
would, in his words, "amaze indeed / The very faculties of eyes and ears."

In the stage world characterized by the careful observation of sight and
sound, Claudius works invisibly, by poison — poison in the ear that
leaves no sign of its entry, poison on the foil that leaves no trace. The
very act of poisoning that we see him perpetrate is to the eye a disappearing act — he dissolves a pearl in a cup of wine. The impalpable testimony
of the ghost points to the invisible crime of Claudius. The false seeming
of a corrupt court is a commonplace of revenge drama, but the necessity
of making visible the verbal truth of the ghost in order to verify it is un-
paralleled. [11] In the course of the play, evidence of the crime is unearthed
that is accessible to the public senses. Until that time, the invisible world
imposed on the visible one makes of Denmark a waking nightmare. [12]

What does it mean for Hamlet to fear his dreams? He speaks of
dreams but gives no inkling of their contents. He seems to dread the
dreamlike quality of perception rather than any image evoked in dream.
What after all could be worse that the waking images of incest, regicide,
and betrayal that pervade the court? Hamlet's dialogue with Rosencrantz
and Guildenstern associates dreams with his feelings of imprisonment
and enclosure. "Denmark's a prison," he tells Rosencrantz. And if
Rosencrantz and Guildenstern think not so, "there is nothing either good
or bad but thinking makes it so." Accused by his old schoolmates of
ambition, he offers:

> O God, I could be bounded in a nutshell, and
> count myself a king of infinite space — were it not that I
> have bad dreams.

                                                            (II.ii.254–56)

In passing, Hamlet offers his schoolmates metaphoric language drawn from the lively Renaissance debate concerning the boundedness of space. (Hamlet seemingly opts with Giordano Bruno and William Gilbert for infinite space.)[13] Hamlet speaks candidly, making no pretense of madness. The conversation takes a seemingly playful turn, but Rosencrantz and Guildenstern continue to probe for some clear declaration of Hamlet's ambitions. He in contrast gives the paradoxes they toy with a more metaphysical turn.

> *Guildenstern.* Which dreams indeed are ambition, for the very substance of the ambitious is merely the shadow of a dream.
>
> *Hamlet.* A dream itself is but a shadow.
>
> *Rosencrantz.* Truly, and I hold ambition of so airy and light a quality that it is but a shadow's shadow.
>
> *Hamlet.* Then are our beggars bodies and our monarchs and outstretched heroes the beggar's shadows. Shall we to th' court? for, by my fay, I cannot reason. (II.ii.257–65)

He presently offers the pair an opportunity to confess that they have been sent for. In this context it seems evident that the "bad dreams," associated in part with social hierarchies, are his waking perception of the world around him, and that his feeling of confinement is akin to his feeling "most dreadfully attended." This perception dominates his stay at Elsinore between the ghost's first appearance and his own sea voyage.

In his discussion of space as a phenomenon of perception, Merleau-Ponty traces the altered sense of space produced by night, dream, and madness in a manner that parallels in some interesting ways Hamlet's perceptions of space in the course of the play. Night as darkness is the most elementary disruption of the spatial sense.

> When, for example, the world of clear and articulate objects is abolished, our perceptual being, cut off from its world, evolves a spatiality without things. This is what happens in the night. Night is not an object before me; it enwraps me and infiltrates through all my senses, stifling my recollections and almost destroying my personal identity. I am no longer withdrawn into my perceptual look-out from which I watch the outlines of objects moving by at a distance. Night has no outlines; it is itself in contact with me and its unity is the mystical unity of the "mana." Even shouts or a distant light people it

only vaguely, and then it comes to life in its entirety; it is pure depth without foreground or background, without surfaces and without any distance separating it from me. All space for the reflecting mind is sustained by thinking which relates its parts to each other, but in this case the thinking starts from nowhere. On the contrary, it is from the heart of nocturnal space that I become united with it. The distress felt by neuropaths in the night is caused by the fact that it brings home to us our contingency, the uncaused and tireless impulse which drives us to seek an anchorage and to surmount ourselves in things, without any guarantee that we shall always find them. [14]

The disruption of Hamlet's world at the beginning of the play is so complete that he welcomes the opportunity to reconstitute it in the night as he would reconstitute the very shapes of things; he wishes his own "too too sallied flesh would melt, / Thaw, and resolve itself into a dew!" The threat of a ghost on the battlements provides him with a release of pent-up energies. He is not concerned that the boundaries of the walls are hidden in night and that the spirit might, as Horatio fears, "tempt [him] toward the flood.... Or to the dreadful summit of the cliff." The terrors of the topography, enhanced by night, cannot threaten him. In Horatio's description:

> The very place puts toys of desperation,
> Without more motive, into every brain
> That looks so many fadoms to the sea
> And hears it roar beneath.
>
> (I.iv.75–78)

In this terrain, Hamlet acts: "Unhand me, gentlemen. / By heaven, I'll make a ghost of him that lets me!"

Hamlet's second significant action in the darkness of night, narrated to Horatio in Act V, occurs on shipboard.

> Up from my cabin,
> My sea-gown scarf'd about me, in the dark
> Grop'd I to find out them, had my desire,
> Finger'd their packet, and in fine withdrew
> To mine own room again, making so bold,
> My fears forgetting manners, to unseal
> Their grand commission ...
>
> (V.ii.12–18)

Disturbed by "a kind of fighting" in his heart, Hamlet gropes through the darkness to find the commission for his death in England. As on the battlements, Hamlet finds the power to act in an enveloping darkness of which he is the center. Unanchored in things, he acts best when the solidity of things dissolves. In contrast, his adversary Claudius is defined by his place in the world as King and as husband. When the Mousetrap play presents him with an image of himself as murderer and usurper, he calls for light to reestablish the world in which he has authority.

Despite his power during the darkness that dissolves form, Hamlet fears what Merleau-Ponty calls the "more striking experience of unreality" that constitutes dream. "During sleep," Merleau-Ponty suggests, "I hold the world present to me only in order to keep it at a distance, and I revert to the subjective sources of my existence."[15] In the darkness, the world is still palpable and explorable; dreams are subjectivity without the opportunity to act. The association of dreams with enclosure that was observed earlier may be explained in part by their common quality of powerlessness. Merleau-Ponty, closely following the literature of psychology, examines the disruption of feelings about space in mental patients. "Beside the physical and geometrical distance which stands between myself and things, a 'lived' distance binds me to things which count and exist for me, and links them to each other." The disruption of this space may be characteristic of schizophrenia: "The shrinkage of lived space, which leaves no margin to the patient, leaves no room for chance" (286). In a similar way, the prison that is Denmark is created by events which focus all Hamlet's attention there and which link the significant people in his world in conspiracy against him, narrowing the boundaries of his "lived space."

Act V disrupts the circumstances of confinement that narrow the world. When Hamlet leaves for England, scrutiny is effectively ended. Laertes, returning from France to avenge his father, is completely satisfied with Claudius's explanation of his role in the death. Ophelia's madness is accepted as a matter of fact. Hamlet's absence leaves Elsinore with nothing that need be observed, but on his return he will enter a different kind of space. Polonius is dead before Hamlet departs; Rosencrantz and Guildenstern leave with him and will not return. The conspiracy against Hamlet is no longer tightly knit; even Laertes, acting as assassin, is ambivalent about his task. Hamlet reenters an Elsinore in which his time is limited by the return of messengers from England, but his space, as defined by the collection of people who inhabit it, is less circumscribed: the agents of espionage have vanished. That Horatio is more prominent lessens Hamlet's terrible isolation. Hamlet's readiness is a consequence of his learning to regard the world as more complex and hence psychologically larger than he had previously imagined. His rescue by pirates opens the closed world of Elsinore to possibilities beyond itself. Ultimately, when Fortinbras enters, Elsinore rejoins the world. In this final act of the play there are no night scenes. There are neither dreams nor nightmare visions of the world. Horatio's goodnight sends Hamlet to a sleep of death that we are no longer enjoined to fear.

The protagonist's return to a normal relationship to space reactivates the spectator's normal relationship to the horizontal plane that is the stage. That is, as Rudolf Arnheim observes, the spectator views the horizontal stage as occupying the dimension in which we commonly act.[16] Having viewed the stage for several hours as a space in which Hamlet does not act, the spectator is to some extent relieved at the return to a territorial struggle. Signs that Elsinore is Claudius's territory are diminished in the last act. Claudius is onstage, with Hamlet absent for only five lines of Act V. Hamlet makes the graveyard his own through establishing his relationship to the deceased Yorick, and he even claims rights equal to those of Laertes at Ophelia's grave site. Within the palace, in the scene of the duel, Hamlet establishes himself in the stage space, his walking place, and agrees to fence with Laertes if the King and his party come to him. After the King's entourage enters, nothing that ensues suggests that Claudius is able to limit Hamlet's physical actions or in fact exercise control over anyone within the space. Laertes confesses; Gertrude drinks from the poisoned cup; Hamlet is able both to stab Claudius and to pour wine down his throat.

At the play's end, all the significant characters, with the exception of Horatio, who remains as record of the events, are dead. In the absence of any personal feeling for the political situation, an audience perceives the place defined by the characters as vacant and thus a logical place for Fortinbras to occupy. The incestuous crimes of the play are unlikely to generate xenophobia. In fact, the pattern of the play suggests that a heroic act is more likely to occur when someone arrives rather than when he remains. Fortinbras finds the space small for a scene of carnage that would better become a battlefield. But he is a stranger to Elsinore.

Hamlet's patterns of perception pose some interesting problems for stage representation. The representation of darkness is fundamentally antithetical to the process of spectatorship. At the risk of belaboring the obvious, we may observe that while the private theaters were able to make use of the psychological effects of actual darkness, the open-air public theater had no means of varying light levels. In practice, this makes comparatively little difference because darkness must in general be represented rather than presented to an audience. The actual darkness of indoor theaters primarily affords the opportunity for high contrast lighting rather than simple darkness.[17]

Shakespeare certainly made no attempt to avoid night scenes, which dominate such diverse plays as *A Midsummer Night's Dream* and *Macbeth*, and control the climaxes of *Romeo and Juliet* and *Othello*, to cite only a few of the more prominent examples. It is probable that night scenes were enacted by coupling the verbal evocation of darkness with the marginal help of such emblematic props as lanterns, torches, or candles.[18] There is no more intrinsic difficulty in representing the effect of darkness than in representing the effects of heat or cold, fatigue or age, eagerness or reluctance. All these effects, whether they result from external or internal causes, can be expressed through bodily gesture. Indeed, our human habit of perpetual small talk about inner and outer weather lends a considerable verisimilitude to such performances. The night, in particular, brings characteristic stage activities: clandestine deeds, wary watching, confused searching, or drunken carousing, to suggest a few that figure prominently in Elizabethan drama.

What is unusual about *Hamlet* is not its use of night settings on an open-air stage but its protagonist's inversion of the normal relationship to darkness: his investment of daytime with the quality of nightmare and night with some measure of freedom to act. The normal constraints that darkness places on behavior and that would be incorporated in the representation of darkness on the stage would not seem to apply to Hamlet himself. The events in *Hamlet* that take place at night reflect this difference.

The scenes on the battlements reflect the most normal staging of night because there are a number of characters present whose normal reactions define the time of day. The notorious anxiety of the soldiers at their watch and Horatio's caution constitute the expected nocturnal gestures. Moreover, the presence of the ghost, a clear enough sign of night, is reinforced by Hamlet's comments on the King's nightly revelry. Hamlet's own anomalous confidence is thus conspicuously displayed, but it creates no confusion.

The second significant representation of night occurs on the occasion of the Mousetrap play. What is unusual here is that we have no clear verbal indicators of darkness until the conclusion of the Mousetrap, when we are enjoined to consider it the witching time of night. The day's affairs are to be completed before the principals head off to bed. The ghost will appear again. But because Hamlet is so active in these scenes, and because everyone else is focused on him, the time of day becomes almost circumstantial. Hamlet's response to the night paradoxically undermines the representation of night. The Freudian reading of the play that provoked the introduction of a bed into Gertrude's closet actually helped to reestablish the time of day.

The third major representation of night is displaced entirely from the stage. Hamlet narrates his shipboard experiences to Horatio. This displacement is the logical consequence of the reversal of polarities of night and day in the play. Hamlet's possession of himself ultimately demands his possession of the day. The violent and perverse events which conclude the play are thus thrust into the light of day.

Whereas the dramaturgy of revenge tragedy in general strongly confirms society's prohibition of revenge, that of *Hamlet* at the very least renders the issue (in context) problematic and for some critics, such as Norman Rabkin, the very model of a drama of unresolvable philosophical conflicts. Shakespeare's control of the significance of space in the play is a major factor in aligning the perception of the spectator. That Hamlet feels less constricted in space as certainly as Macbeth feels increasingly enclosed by an approaching Birnan (Birnam) wood aligns the audience toward him in an essentially positive way. The extent to which this counterbalances the ideological presuppositions of the audience will vary with the audience. For Francis Barker, for example, the Hamlet of Act V is a "second Hamlet" and "the challenge of his incipient modernity is extinguished." But the examination of his relation to the stage space allows us a means to suggest that his stillness represents a greater potential energy than his previous verbal incisiveness. In describing Shakespeare's spatial choices within the range of Elizabethan norms for such choices as well as establishing an abstract diachronic context for examining the definition of space in drama, we do the study of Elizabethan culture no injustice. If we observe that Shakespearean tragedies refer spectators less consistently (or, at the very least, less simply) to social norms of value than do Shakespeare's history plays, we are justified in investigating the ways in which his plays control spectators' perceptions.[19]

Hamlet was written not only with the theater in mind but with a particular stage space at hand together with particular conventions of representation. Under these circumstances we can see the text as defining a relationship of action to space. While the play allows, even demands, creativity in performance, it determines spatial choices — and other choices, which we shall see — for any performance presenting itself as a performance of *Hamlet*. The study of ways in which the text projects itself into the theater suggests that our interest in the play as performed will not alienate us from the text. The study of the macrostructures of scenic space undertaken here suggests a kind of study which narrows the gap between the text and the semiology of performance.[20]

2
Taking Up the Past:
Hamlet and Time

In twentieth-century drama, the act of waiting has become almost a genre in itself. Beckett's *Godot*, Sartre's *No Exit*, and their dramatic progeny ask an audience to focus on the process of duration as the consciousness perceives it. Although the theatrical tempo of Shakespeare's play would never be mistaken for that of Beckett's, *Hamlet* makes a similar demand.[1] In *Hamlet*, however, duration as a distinct issue must be extracted from a network of questions about time that occur regularly in the critical tradition concerning both *Hamlet* and the Shakespearean canon at large.

A criticism aware of Shakespeare's stage practice has accustomed us to balance the demands of theatrical tempo with the demands of plausible chronology. We expect an acceleration of events and agree to overlook minor inconsistencies. We are accustomed as well to Shakespeare's assessment of human life within a Renaissance value system, where time is a measure of growth or decay in the individual or society, as in *Troilus and Cressida* and *Richard II*.[2] But when the action imitated is the act of hesitation, we are not concerned with time as a way of keeping track of events but with the consciousness as a repository of duration. Hesitation increases the duration of an act, focusing attention not on the rearrangement of the world achieved by an action, but on the action as a movement through time.[3]

No Shakespearean play resists the reduction of time to a spatial analogue as completely as does *Hamlet*. And most of what we value in *Hamlet* depends on the distinction. Throughout the action of the play,

47

Hamlet moves as quickly as his antagonists. Only his consciousness of duration tells him that their combat is taking place in slow motion. Hamlet agonizes over the pace of things because time matters to the human consciousness. Henri Bergson's well-known distinction between time experienced as duration and time conceptualized in spatial terms points toward a way of distinguishing the treatment of time in purely textual literature from the use of time in dramatic texts written with the expectation of theatrical performance.[4] Bergson remains more popular with literary critics than with philosophers. Philosophical objections to Bergson's view stem in part from his assumption that space is objectified before perception. If we go beyond him it must be in the direction of linking both space and time to perception.[5]

When we speak of dramatic form, we necessarily do so by means of a spatial description, which has been called a "heuristic metaphor animated by our intensely felt need to order the chaos of reality."[6] The spatial metaphor expresses a sense of control. Yet in the complementary experience of felt chaos, the disposition to the spatial metaphor remains so strong that we typically express chaos as a failure of vision. The moral confusion of John Webster's plays characteristically culminates in metaphors of obscured sight. In *The White Devil*, a dying Vittoria laments, "My soule, like to a ship in a black storme, / Is driven I know not whither" (V.vi.5–6). Her brother Flamineo, dying with her, negates history, "I doe not looke / Who went before, nor who shall follow mee; / Noe, at my selfe I will begin and end" (V.vi.15–17).[7] Our customary use of words seems inevitably to evoke space. Shakespeare expresses the power whereby the mind inquires into past and future in similar visual terms. For Hamlet, "He that made us with such large discourse, / Looking before and after, gave us not / That capability and Godlike reason / To fust in us unus'd" (IV.iv.36–39). Discourse creates visual images of time, but drama has at its disposal a means other than language to convey the inalienable subjectivity of time: the potential to control and segment the presentation of events during the time of performance.

The representation of phenomena in the theater is obviously unlike representation through a text in that the stage has at its disposal space and objects, and in that real time elapses as a performance takes place. Although the purposes of drama are usually served by a space similar, at least in its dimensions, to the places we normally inhabit, time is generally compressed.

The compression of time is generally achieved by means of two devices: an extraordinary concurrence of events and the insertion of gaps in the representation of time. The concentration of events in a short period of time (implicit compression) is not in itself a violation of the expectations of the audience. But because the concurrence of events is a structural characteristic of the climax of drama, a play that relies heavily on this device, *Oedipus Rex* for example, tends to seem all climax. More commonly, compression is explicit: action is accelerated by gaps in the time scheme of the plot, which may be used to accentuate significant sequences of events or which may themselves be significant. When, as occurs frequently in Shakespeare's complex plots, the alternation of scenes from independent chains of events deliberately distracts attention from time or disrupts time,[8] duration is not an issue. But, alternatively, a gap in time may be emphasized to demonstrate changes in character which constitute the internal effects of what has transpired. In types of drama sufficiently traditional that the term character makes sense, an Aristotelian distinction is normally appropriate: a character who changes must show that change by making choices differently as a result of the assimilation of experience. It must take some stage time to establish that a change in behavior has occurred. One natural consequence of the disruption of events by time gaps is that both as audience and, in a more leisurely way, as analysts, we reconstitute a story from the plot. (The *fabula/sjuzet* distinction of the Russian formalists is the most potent modern formulation of this traditional act.)[9] In drama, the plot as acted text subordinates the story reconstituted from the plot to a greater degree than a narrated plot can subordinate the story it implies.

Modern theatrical practice has been intensely concerned with conveying immediacy, the moment-by-moment quality of experience. Dramatic theory shares this concern. Comedy permits and even encourages digression, but in a tragedy we attend to each moment with the implicit promise that it is significantly related to an imminent future. In Susanne Langer's terms, "literature creates a virtual past, drama creates a virtual future."[10] If this concern with the moment is acknowledged, the craft of the playwright must balance the need for scope with the necessity of expressing immediacy through stretches of continuous time. For neoclassical theorists, continuity is a necessary element of dramatic illusion, but the value of continuity does not depend on the assumption that theater is illusion. In a manner more compatible with Elizabethan theater, the modern focus on the experience of the audience preserves a sense of the actor's identity as distinct from that of the character. Herbert Blau formulates the conception eloquently.

> The critical thing, then, in the institution of theater is not so much that an actor is there, but that an actor is so vulnerably there. Whatever he represents in the play, in the order of time he is representing nobody but himself. How could he? That's his body, doing time. [11]

Although theater criticism like that of Blau is often anti-text, it describes, I believe, the climate of expectation that dominates our choice of those texts, in the performance of which we continue to be actively interested, and in the analysis of which we continue to be actively engaged. Stephen Booth, for example, correlates the temporal reality of audience experience with the text of *Hamlet* in asserting that the audience "gets information or sees action it once wanted only after a new interest has superseded the old."[12]

In its consistent concern with duration itself, *Hamlet* demands our attention to almost all the difficulties that the representation of time can create in the theater. The audience must accept for itself the task of understanding a protagonist for whom timing is essential and whose subjective sense of time changes as the play unfolds. Given the rapid tempo resulting from dramatic compression, the audience gropes for ways to assess Hamlet's judgment. Quantitative measure of time expressed in words is of little help. Early in the play, two months is a measure of extraordinary haste when it refers to Gertrude's remarriage, and of extraordinary hesitation when it refers to Hamlet's failure to avenge his father's death. Yet in Act V, Hamlet feels that an interim of a few days is sufficient time for whatever he must undertake.

Conflicting indications of Hamlet's age have sufficiently complicated the assessment of Hamlet's behavior as to have created virtually an open house for psychological critics. Hamlet's actions have been assessed against norms ranging from those appropriate to Hamlet's adolescent behavior to those appropriate for mature behavior. Immature Hamlets are viewed as confounding the problems of normal development with those of his particular predicament. Older Hamlets seem unnaturally powerless. However, a larger issue — how the past and future impinge upon the present — directs the audience away from the limitations of regarding Hamlet as defined by any single stage in the process of maturation.

Disturbed by an event in the past, his father's murder, and by a responsibility to avenge himself on his uncle in the future, Hamlet is incapable
of acting decisively in the present. When he accepts that past and future,
he possesses the present. Because this broader philosophical issue
overrides, to some extent, decisions concerning Hamlet's age, the
Hamlets of the theater do not diverge as widely as might otherwise be
expected.

The play's chronology is an inevitable reference point for the discussion of time. *Hamlet* transpires in less than a year's time: soldiers
complain of the bitter cold as the play begins; Ophelia drowns while
gathering flowers just before the play ends. But for the bulk of the play
the sense of season is muted; very little awareness of natural time
penetrates to the interior of Elsinore. The play begins less than two
months after Hamlet Senior's death (Act I); shifts to an interlude of some
week's time four months after the death (II-IV.iii); accounts briefly for
events in Hamlet's absence (IV.iv-vii); and concludes swiftly after his
return from the sea, perhaps a month later (Act V). This chronology
would suggest that the play presents the last year of a Hamlet who we are
told is thirty years old in the graveyard scene. Within the longer framework, Hamlet's stage appearances represent three short periods of time
separated by significant gaps after his confrontation with the ghost
(between Acts I and II) and during his sea voyage (after IV.iii). Harley
Granville-Barker's perception of what he terms the three movements of
the play, created by these gaps, has stood the test of time as a guide to the
theatrical rhythm of the play.[13] Each of these gaps may be seen not
merely as a compression of the action but as a significant duration during
which Hamlet's attitude toward time can be seen to have changed. (In
both instances, onstage action clearly establishes the time lapse before
Hamlet appears.) In each of the three phases of his experience he is retrospective, but only in the final phase can his retrospection embrace more
than the immediate past, and only in this last phase is his view of present
and future undistorted by his retrospection.

In no other Shakespearean tragedy does the action of the play depend
so heavily upon the protagonist's response to an event conceived as
having transpired before the play begins.[14] Hamlet's dialogue with the
past explores the multiple consequences of a crime far more economical
in the doing than in the undoing. In the ghost's words, he was "Of life, of
crown, of queen, at once dispatch'd." Hamlet mourns for his father, feels

his flesh sullied by his mother's hasty remarriage, despises the person of
Claudius, regrets the crime of incest, and perceives himself to have been
cheated of the crown. Assimilating the consequences of the murder
requires a far longer duration than the act of committing it. Merleau-
Ponty's observations on the difficulty of introducing historicity into the
events of life suggest some of the problems of coming to terms with the
crime.

> My hold on the past and the future is precarious, and my possession of my
> own time is always postponed until a stage when I may fully understand it,
> yet this stage can never be reached, since it would be one more moment,
> bounded by the horizon of its future, and requiring in its turn future develop-
> ments in order to be understood. (346)

The tragic protagonist, if he is granted a moment of recognition, is
characteristically able to resolve the interaction of past and future when
the events of the past determine his personal future, traditionally the
circumstances and significance of his death. At the beginning of the play,
the difficult process of possessing his own time has not yet been simpli-
fied for Hamlet by imminent death, and an enormous burden of past
events bears upon his present. As a consequence, not only is Hamlet lost
in deliberation, but his antagonists are deprived of the opportunity to
oppose him in a dialogue that concerns his real objectives. The closet
scene with Gertrude interrupts this introspection, and the sea voyage
seems to end it, but the beginning of the play displays the structural
peculiarity of a protagonist whose internal focus disengages the other
characters of the play from the core of its action.

In no action within the drama is Hamlet's antagonist Claudius
efficient: his stratagems are foiled; his agents are inefficient; his
conscience is strong enough to trouble him, but too weak to accomplish
his salvation. Hamlet wins the stage encounter: his living presence in
Elsinore taints Claudius's victory. He taunts Claudius, threatens him, and
evokes his sense of guilt. As his father's namesake, Hamlet evokes an
even stronger than usual sense of the father surviving in the son. Hamlet
achieves his minor objectives as Claudius does not, yet each triumph
renews Hamlet's despair. As Hamlet's certainty of the depravity of the
present increases, his despair at being unable to redeem the time deepens.
Time "out of joint" is dislocated history: every bit of evidence that
increases Hamlet's certainty of the guilt of the King increases as well his

awareness of the rift created by the King's crime. Hamlet's capacity for action in the present is undermined by his own successful inquiry into the past.

The first problem in analyzing Hamlet's relationship with the past arises through the initial conditions of the play. These conditions define the immediate past and provide indications of Hamlet's age. Hamlet's presence at Wittenberg suggests an age closer to twenty years than to the thirty years that Act V suggests. As readers, if not as playgoers, we have evolved ways to avoid being troubled by these boundaries. We allow the contradictory indicators of age to suggest attitudes toward Hamlet: a sense of the burden placed on extreme youth in the beginning; a sense of his manhood and sufficiency in the end.[15] Difficulties arise when we look for the psychological causes of Hamlet's reaction to his situation, by which we mean the psychological models for the imitation of behavior or personality that we find in the play.[16]

The difficulty does not simply disappear when we change nomenclature, demanding of dramatic imitation something less consistent than case history. Hamlet must still be acted. And he will probably be presented as a rebellious youth in one playhouse and an indecisive entrant to middle age in another for as long as the play is performed. Psychoanalysis tugs the representation toward adolescence while the economics of the theater thrusts to the fore middle-aged actors with box office clout. But Shakespeare is not merely an innocent victim of a struggle for precision alien to Elizabethan theater conditions. He has posited a Hamlet whose relationship to Ophelia throughout the play generates concerns appropriate to the young lover, whereas his process of coming to terms with mortality suggests an older man. But because the sexual dimension of the usurper's crime — incestuous marriage with Gertrude — yokes sexuality with mortality in the central issue of the play, Hamlet is never exclusively concerned with the problems particular to a single age for a sustained period of time.

The initial circumstances of the play suggest problems more extensive than the conflicting indications of Hamlet's age. If Hamlet returned from Wittenberg when his father died, then the earnest wooing of Ophelia that alarmed Polonius and Laertes would be assumed to have occurred in the immediate aftermath of the funeral. It would be difficult to envision how he could have wooed her during this hypothetical period of time, but the consequences of the relationship are obvious enough. A father places obstacles in the way of his daughter's suitor. This simple situation is compounded by the naive complicity of the father with the murderer of the suitor's father. The suitor's consequent emotional confusion, rather than a clear sequence of events that would have precipitated it, is what the situation requires. From a critical standpoint we must be aware that though the presumed hiatus at Wittenberg explains many of Hamlet's characteristics, there are equally many characteristics, as suitor and courtier, that would be precluded by his having spent most of his time at a foreign university. The combined effect of these alternative personal histories is to make Hamlet a stranger to Elsinore even as he is intimately involved with it. His double past complicates our perception of even those relationships not directly affected by his father's death.

Wittenberg is not merely a sign of youth but also a qualification to think seriously about metaphysics. On the battlements, Horatio is nominated by the soldiers to speak to the ghost because he is a scholar. Hamlet's own physical daring on the battlements depends upon his argument that his soul is safe: "What can [the ghost] do to that, / Being a thing immortal as itself?" Both scholars are assumed to be versed in what their world knows of speculative creatures like ghosts. Because the scholarship of Horatio and Hamlet makes them more ready than soldiers to encounter the other world, Wittenberg evokes a kind of experience rather than a kind of inexperience.

Hamlet's wooing of Ophelia far more clearly suggests his youth. Polonius is concerned particularly with the dishonor Ophelia might encounter when "the blood burns."

> These blazes, daughter,
> Giving more light than heat, extinct in both
> Even in their promise, as it is a-making,
> You must not take for fire....
>
> . . . .
> ... For Lord Hamlet,
> Believe so much in him, that he is young,
> And with a larger teder may he walk
> Than may be given you.
>
> (I.iii.117–20, 123–26)

This assumption that intense desire is naturally linked to youth is sustained beyond Act I. Hamlet upbraids his mother in her closet for having committed her crime of incest at an age when "the heyday in the blood is tame, it's humble, / And waits upon the judgment." That the sexual crimes of the play are committed by the old makes them more heinous, at least to the young.

> O shame, where is thy blush?
> Rebellious hell,
> If thou canst mutine in a matron's bones,
> To flaming youth let virtue be as wax
> And melt in her own fire. Proclaim no shame
> When the compulsive ardure gives the charge,
> Since frost itself as actively doth burn,
> And reason panders will.
>
> (III. iv.81–88)

The contrast between young and old focuses on the balance between reason and the ardor of the blood rather than on experience. It is not because the old have learned in the course of time to be wise, but because their physical capacity for passion has diminished, that they are assumed to be capable of controlling their sexual impulses.

Hamlet ignores gradations of age: significant characters are either of Hamlet's generation or of his mother's. For the difference between twenty and thirty to be significant in assessing Hamlet, the play would have to focus on some experience that ought to occur in this decade. Hamlet's not having entered the fullness of royal responsibility may more reasonably be attributed to his father's continued reign than to the kind of dereliction we find in Prince Hal. Aside from the responsibility to succeed his father, Hamlet has, as prince in a country not at war, no public obligation. Nor can we expect the marriage of a royal prince to take place simply because he is old enough to head a household.

Hamlet's denoted age at his death, the thirty years since his birth referred to in the graveyard scene, is no more reliable than the expected age of an undergraduate as the source of a norm for Hamlet's behavior in the play. The same time reference would make "young Fortinbras," whose father was slain by Hamlet Senior on Hamlet's birthday, at least thirty. Yet Fortinbras is, in Hamlet's terms, "a delicate and tender prince" whose ambition spurs Hamlet's own "dull revenge." If the martial prowess of Fortinbras has the effect of making him a foil to the hesitant Hamlet, Hamlet's age can hardly be the issue. Nor could Hamlet be more than a few years older than Laertes, another foil, who had warned his sister of the dangers of Hamlet's youth. Each of the three — Hamlet, Fortinbras, and Laertes — is viewed as a youth, and each seems to under-take his first significant public act during the play. The play ultimately refers us to its internal gaps in time as the only significant durations subject to analysis.

When critics remark that Hamlet castigates himself for inactivity while an audience finds him feverishly active, they are inevitably referring to the second phase of the play.[17] All of the stage encounters between Hamlet and the court subsequent to the ghost's revelation and before the sea voyage transpire within the space of a few days at most. The lapse of time before this action is fixed by Ophelia's comment at the Mousetrap play; it is "twice two months" since Hamlet Senior's death, hence two or three months after Hamlet vowed revenge. Ophelia's reference is consis-tent with other time references in this section of the play (II.i-IV.iv). Polonius is sending a spy to inquire after Laertes' reputation in Paris, which we must assume he has taken some time to establish. The ambas-sadors to Norway have left, negotiated, and returned. Hamlet's unusual behavior has been noted; Rosencrantz and Guildenstern have been sent for and they have arrived. The length of time occupied by this phase of the action is most clearly indicated to the audience by the activities of the players, who arrive at Elsinore and rehearse and stage a play. Hamlet's departure for England in IV.iv crosses Fortinbras's army for what must be judged as thematic convenience. (They should not be there so soon.) But on the whole, the chronology in this passage is consistent, and the lapse of time since Hamlet vowed revenge is not merely denoted by a single reference but emphasized for an audience by the comings and goings on the stage.

Thus, a large part of the hesitation for which Hamlet criticizes himself is not time we experience as an audience but time between the scenes which is brought to our attention by Hamlet's self-reproach and by the stage devices which indicate that time has passed. James Calderwood has explored the devices of Shakespeare's craft which make present this absence of action, a process he denotes "Naming of Delay/Naming as Delay."[18] He notes the power of language to create a "caesural pres-ence," which must nonetheless yield to drama's "essential nature as a performance in time" (148). In the terms generated by linguistic theory, Calderwood explores Hamlet's resistance to an inevitably suicidal diachronic movement (action), a resistance which is also *Hamlet*'s resistance to an inevitably "theatricidal" diachronic movement (performance).

Critical attempts to provide reasons for Hamlet's hesitation are deprived of evidence outside his own consciousness. The analysis is further baffled by the play's metatheatrical naming of its own delay. More directly subject to scrutiny than the process of hesitation are the actions Hamlet undertakes when he spurs himself to activity. He approaches his task by indirection and he may be accused of playing a kind of "Achilles and the tortoise" game, constructing a series of actions that approach the killing of Claudius but never attain it. Does not the Hamlet of Act I seem certain enough of his father's murder not to require the Mousetrap play to test the King's conscience? What blunts the purpose that seemed so strong?

Until the last act of the play, Hamlet's behavior is most influenced by what is immediate in his memory. In Act I his memory is focused on his father as he was when living. His most tortured memories are of his mother's devotion to his father, and his awareness of Claudius in the present is dominated by his comparison of Claudius to his father. But at the end of the time gap between Acts I and II, Hamlet's memory is focused on the events of Act I. His father as ghost in his memory (and in actuality) reminds him of his duty to revenge, but his father as ghost is not identical in his mind with his father as he lived. The ghost is an occult phenomenon whose request will be obeyed if his message is true, and Hamlet's initial attitude to the ghost is only partially filial. The possibility that the apparition is diabolical informs his first words to the ghost.

> Angels and ministers of grace defend us!
> Be thou a spirit of health, or goblin damn'd,
> Bring with thee airs from heaven, or blasts from hell,
> Be thy intents wicked, or charitable,
> Thou com'st in such a questionable shape
> That I will speak to thee. I'll call thee Hamlet,
> King, father, royal Dane.

> (I.iv.39–45)

Hamlet's resolution is momentary. Both "spirit of health" and "goblin damn'd" remain psychological realities, and the ghostly father is never identical with the remembered father until the two images are reconciled by the appearance of the ghost in the role of devoted husband in the closet scene. As long as all the nurturing impulses of the father are associated with his father in memory and the aggressive impulses associated with his father as ghost, Hamlet seemingly cannot reconcile that part of himself that heals with that part which wills to destroy. In the closet scene, Hamlet holds his father's portrait in his hand yet invokes the protective wings of "heavenly guards" when his father's apparition appears. When he appears in Gertrude's closet, however, the ghost devotes fewer words to urging revenge against Claudius than to confining Hamlet's anger against his mother to moral persuasion.

> Do not forget! This visitation
> Is but to whet thy almost blunted purpose.
> But look, amazement on thy mother sits,
> O, step between her and her fighting soul.
> Conceit in weakest bodies strongest works,
> Speak to her, Hamlet.
>
> (III.iv.110–16)

After this appearance, his last, there is no further evidence of a split between ghost and father in Hamlet's mind. Hamlet adopts the struggle against Claudius as his own. Images of the father, not the questionable ghost, dominate his memory. In his retrospective self-reproach, "How all occasions do inform against me," he urges himself to action by citing his having suffered "a father kill'd, a mother stain'd." On his subsequent return from the trip to England, he recounts having used his father's signet ring to seal the fate of Rosencrantz and Guildenstern. He is later able to see the parallel between his troubles and those of Laertes: both have lost Ophelia and a father. When Hamlet is finally able to view what has happened to him as removed from the realm of the preternatural, the human experience of loss has displaced the unnatural visitation which revealed the crime. Until the father is viewed in memory as a single figure, the past remains problematic, and action in the present is inhibited. [19]

The models of human perception proposed by modern phenomenologists are particularly appropriate to the description of Hamlet because they view time as a continuous process of becoming. Through the human consciousness, the past is focused on action in the future. Merleau-Ponty describes perception of the present thus: "A present without a future, or an eternal present, is precisely the definition of death; the living present is torn between a past which it takes up and a future which it projects."[20] Objectively, Hamlet's ability to make use of time does not vary a great deal in the course of the play. What does vary is the degree to which Hamlet is willing to "take up" the past and to "project" a future. The play constructs a Hamlet whose "restricted present" early in the play consti- tutes a kind of living death in Merleau-Ponty's terms and whose "full present" in Act V constitutes a return to life even when his death is imminent. [21]

Hamlet's most strained reasoning occurs in the vast middle passage of the play that represents so few days (II-IV.iii), and it is here that we find the heightening of his consciousness that constitutes the painful "eternal present." The Mousetrap provides Hamlet with evidence vital to assimi- lating the ghost's message, but almost immediately thereafter he decides not to kill the praying Claudius. Retrospectively, Hamlet perceives his thoughts to have been three parts coward and one part wisdom. In the midst of things he observes that "conscience does make cowards of us all." The term "conscience" implied, to the Elizabethans, consciousness as well as conscience (as in contemporary French), and the complexities of the word are significant.

"Conscience," on the occasions when it inhibits Hamlet, is not simply awareness of moral laws but also fear of conjectured possibilities. The mere possibility that the ghost is diabolical inhibits Hamlet's impulse to revenge.

> The spirit that I have seen
> May be a dev'l, and the dev'l hath power
> T'assume a pleasing shape, yea, and perhaps,
> Out of my weakness and my melancholy,
> As he is very potent with such spirits,
> Abuses me to damn me.
>
> (II.ii.598–603)

Whereas Hamlet's "conscience" explores the hypothetical, the "conscience of the King" which Hamlet will catch is more simply a heightened awareness of past crimes.

"Conscience" as consciousness appears explicitly in the most famous soliloquy, "To be or not to be," where conjecture rather than moral law is sufficient to eliminate suicide as an alternative. The potential of the mind to pose questions that it cannot answer inhibits action. The soliloquy, almost too familiar to need citation, asks "who would bear the whips and scorns of time....

> But that the dread of something after death,
> The undiscover'd country, from whose bourn
> No traveller returns, puzzles the will,
> And makes us rather bear those ills we have,
> Than fly to others that we know not of?
> Thus conscience does make cowards of us all,
> And thus the native hue of resolution
> Is sicklied o'er with the pale cast of thought,
> And enterprises of great pitch and moment
> With this regard their currents turn awry,
> And lose the name of action.

(III.i.77–87)

The passage defies close reading because it reverses the polarity of words. "Time" is merely a quantitative measure of abuse. If "action" means the quest for nonbeing, sleep without dreams, then "enterprise" and "resolution" lead to nothingness and the "pale cast of thought" leads to survival. Speculation produces non-sense.

This crippling capacity to hypothesize peaks in the scene where Hamlet spares Claudius at prayer. Ignoring the more difficult question of whether Hamlet rationalizes to avoid murder in cold blood, we find Hamlet conjecturing about the state of Claudius's soul and that of his own father who has died "full of bread, / With all his crimes broad blown as flush as May." Hamlet's own responsibilities to the Christian code that underlies his theological speculation are unexplored. A refusal to kill that would normally be attributed to "conscience" in the modern sense is here depicted as a product of consciousness.

Whereas Hamlet is incapacitated by conjecture, Claudius is weakened by awareness of past crimes. "Conscience" in Claudius's usage is always a kind of moral accounting. Polonius's platitudinous observation "that with devotion's visage / And pious action we do sugar o'er / The devil himself" provokes the King's guilty response: "How smart a lash that speech doth give my conscience!" His susceptibility to the Mousetrap needs little comment. Hamlet's principal accomplishment before the bloody confrontation of Act V is to bring the crimes of the past into the present through the medium of the King's conscience. Hamlet and the King battle to a standstill, each hampered by his own distinct version of "conscience." The vulnerability of the King's conscience is seemingly ended when Hamlet sheds the blood of Polonius. Claudius's final usage of the term is mere abuse. Cozening Laertes into joining his last plot to murder Hamlet, Claudius appeals to Laertes' moral judgment. "Conscience" is here almost a matter of bookkeeping.

> Now must your conscience my acquittance seal,
> And you must put me in your heart for friend,
> Sith you have heard, and with a knowing ear,
> That he which hath your noble father slain
> Pursued my life.
>
> (IV.vii.1–5)

Hamlet, the most conscious character in dramatic literature, antedates the entry of the term "consciousness" into the English language. The multiple meanings of the term "conscience" veil the essential difference between the effect on Claudius of the memory of past crimes and the effect on Hamlet of the ghost's accusation concerning these same crimes. The middle passage of the play consists largely of Hamlet's coming to terms with the possibilities generated by the ghost's message. Until this resolution, Hamlet's relationship with Ophelia is particularly vexed by the discontinuity of past and present. His ambivalence toward her pervades the play. We hear a doting letter he has written her. She presents a narration of his mimed grief, within the time frame of the play but already in the past when we perceive it. But these events are presented as relics. When we see them together, Hamlet is less loving. He makes Ophelia the subject and audience of a sermon; he subjects her to obscene, or at least inappropriately ribald, banter at the play. After she absents herself by suicide, he professes love, but he does so in a bizarre manner. When he returns to Denmark after her death, he takes offense at her brother's exclamation of love and mocks him with bombastic protestations of his own. But by then their relationship is consigned to the past forever. As audience we are left to imagine the positive aspects of a relationship in which nothing positive occurs onstage during the play.

Hamlet's encounters with Ophelia parallel his soliloquy "To be or not to be" in reflecting his ambivalence toward being. In confronting Ophelia, he questions her "honesty" — chastity as a virtue in itself — but he also cautions her against being "a breeder of sinners." Earlier, in warning Polonius of how his daughter might conceive, he invokes morality but courts nonbeing by denouncing fertility. In contrast, Hamlet's sexual banter at the play, mixed though it is with anger and subterfuge, reflects the active impulse to sexuality, the desire to be and to project a future. In large measure, Ophelia is for Hamlet not a lover but a metaphor for being. His contact with her entire family is distant, his rela- tions with them mere representations of his inner turmoil. The death of Polonius is an accident, but it is the kind of mishap that could only be perpetrated by someone for whom the being of others isn't very real. We can only be astonished at Hamlet's subsequent perplexity that his victim's son feels anger toward him. We perceive Hamlet as a stranger, in part because the play defines him as having been away, but primarily because he defines himself as a stranger to the present, seemingly refus- ing to acknowledge the reality of his own behavior after his father's death.

In the last phase of his experience (Act V), Hamlet gives every indica- tion of having assimilated the past. He conceives of his father as a single entity. He is certain that Claudius is a criminal, and is certain of his own capacity for action. He is even capable of acknowledging how he has wronged Laertes and of perceiving that another can feel as he feels. The sense of urgency that accompanied his fevered and indirect efforts against the crown has been replaced by a sense of having enough time; he perceives the interim as his. His new sense of time is inextricable from his sense of destiny, a sense that the pattern of events seems to validate: he perceives the shape of his own tragedy. "Seeing the pattern" frees the protagonist not from suffering but from confusion about his identity. This liberation is experienced by an audience as spiritual power.

In the events subsequent to his exile, coincidence works for Hamlet rather than against him. Whereas his instinctive stabbing of the figure behind the arras had brought about the unfortunate death of Polonius, all his subsequent instincts are effective and all subsequent accidents serve to purge the kingdom. The high-sounding principle "There's a divinity that shapes our ends, / Rough-hew them how we will" is embedded in nothing more noble than Hamlet's account of how his restlessness at sea led him to open the documents carried by Rosencrantz and Guildenstern, to discover his death sentence there, and to substitute a document sending them to death. The context which is narrated does not suggest religious transcendence, but a sense of harmony is nonetheless evoked by the language and by Hamlet's own sense of well-being at the moment in the play when he narrates the story.

The play's coincidences allow the fundamental conflict between revenge and Christianity to be sidestepped: the active machinations of Claudius ultimately create the tempo of a duel in which stroke and counterstroke follow too swiftly for conscience to intervene. External events relieve Hamlet of much of the burden of choice. Ophelia drowns. Pirates return Hamlet to Elsinore. The King's plan to kill him with a poisoned foil provides a soldierly context for his final struggle. Gertrude drinks from the poisoned cup intended for Hamlet, joining him symbolically if not intentionally. What Hamlet discovers is not an intellectual or theological solution to Denmark's malaise but an ability to recognize and feel a range of distinct emotions. Sorrow at Ophelia's death, regret for his behavior with Laertes, anger at the King, and affection for Horatio are not blurred by his preoccupation with the conflicts within his own mind. Yet his mind is fullest in these moments.

The reach of Hamlet's memory is longest in this final phase: He remembers his own childhood when the grave digger unearths Yorick's skull. Although the graveyard still suggests the paradoxes of mortality, death is both accepted as the human condition and deplored by the living. The skull of Yorick smells of decay, but the memories of Yorick's clowning are sweet. Though the consequences he draws are in the vein of the satirist, Hamlet affirms his childhood affections for the jester.

> Alas, poor Yorick! I knew him Horatio, a
> fellow of infinite jest, of most excellent fancy. He
> hath bore me on his back a thousand times, and now
> how abhorr'd in my imagination it is! my gorge rises
> at it. Here hung those lips that I have kiss'd I know not
> how oft. Where be your gibes now, your gambols,
> your songs, your flashes of merriment, that were
> wont to set the table on a roar? Not one now to mock
> your own grinning — quite chop-fall'n.

(V.i.184–92)

Like his presumed residence at Wittenberg, Hamlet's graveyard contemplation of age, the passage of time, and mortality suggests his potentials rather than defining his limitations. Hamlet's potential for

kingship, later acknowledged by Fortinbras, is evoked by his contemplation of the death of kings. Alexander, at his prime at the age of thirty,
must, Hamlet observes, have become a heap of bones that looked and
smelled like the most common skull in the graveyard. In the general
process of decay, the triumphs of princes wither. The perspective of the
graveyard diminishes the importance of the moment; pain and haste seem
no longer appropriate.[22]

Between the extremes of the shock of sudden death that begins the
play and the inevitability of centuries that turn Caesars to dust stands the
normal mortality of Yorick. The remembrance of things past evoked by
Yorick's skull permits an understanding of the normal pace of time.
When Hamlet was a child, he rode the shoulders of the clown whose
skull he contemplates. The frame of mind in which Hamlet is philosophi-
cally ready to accept death, now or to come, yet feels uneasiness at an
imminent encounter with danger, results from his having understood that
violent death is a special case of human mortality. His ability to feel is
crucial to his humanity: neither shock nor philosophical contemplation
eradicates his sorrow.

Hamlet does not undergo a simple passage from one age of man to
another. Rather, he struggles to reestablish his ability to contemplate both
the past and the possibilities of the future. Trapped as he is in Act I
between horror of the immediate past and dread of the future, Hamlet is
unable to see opportunities for choice in the present. It is necessary that
he regain the fullness of his humanity, memory of the past, and faith in
the future, to evoke in the audience a sense that he is capable of action.
Modern criticism has been too willing to embrace the alienated Hamlet
without seeing that the reconciled Hamlet does not break with the rigor
of the initial conception. Viewing *Hamlet* as a key text in his provocative
study of subjectivity and subjection, Francis Barker, for example, finds
its protagonist to be a discontinuous quasi-Brechtian figure whose
"incipient modernity is extinguished" as he begins to act.[23] My examination argues that the hollow subjectivity that Barker discovers early in the
play occurs because Hamlet is emptied of that which returns to him late
in the play: his own past and future.

In the end, Hamlet is synchronized with the world. In part this occurs
because the play's resolution aligns the actions of protagonist and antagonist in ways that do not mirror our expectations in life. But it is also true
that within the assumed reality of the play, he is seen as using the flow of

events in time to achieve his purposes. He no longer struggles to reject the present time but turns what is to better purpose. Early in the play he is able to improvise by using neutral events, like the arrival of the players, to advantage, but later he turns negatives to advantage. Being kidnapped by pirates, he finds himself safer than before. Quarreling with Laertes, he discovers his own wrong in having killed Polonius.

In Act V, when the King proposes a fencing match, Hamlet feels uneasy: for the first time he acknowledges fear of the future. But at the same time he faces that future, accepting what his intuition suggests will be a struggle to the death.

> Not a whit, we defy augury. There is special
> providence in the fall of a sparrow. If it be now,
> 'tis not to come; if it be not to come, it will be now; if
> it be not now, yet it will come — the readiness is all.
> Since no man, of aught he leaves, knows what is't to
> leave betimes, let be.
>
> (V.ii.219–24)

Hamlet has been reckless in the course of the play, but he has never before been "ready," prepared for the indeterminate. His readiness leads to the death of the usurper Claudius and his own death, perceived as "felicity" in the end. In some alternative time, as Fortinbras conjectures in epitaph, "he was likely, had he been put on, to have proved most royal." In his words, respect for Hamlet's capacity for action is reestablished within the play.

Hamlet's relative youth is not the measure of what is lost in his death. That death reaches with equal significance into both past and future. His potential as king, "had he been put on," is no more valuable than the integrity of his past: his mythic birth on the day of his father's military triumph, his joys in childhood, his place in the scheme of things in young manhood. Ultimately the play demands that we envision not ten years of the hero's life compressed into the span of the play, but life's entirety. The "indefinition" of the loss, to use Booth's term, implies the "sudden invasion of our finite consciousness by the fact of infinite possibility."[24] What we ask of an enactment of Hamlet on the stage is suggested by Hamlet's attitude before his death, vulnerability that is not diminished by increasing wisdom. Thus, we should not be astonished that so many actors so diverse in age have triumphed in the role.

Hamlet is a play in which the protagonist mediates our attitudes toward the action through his control over our sense of time. If we evade his subjective view, as analysis often does, what we analyze is no longer the play we experience. Rather than estrange ourselves from this experience, we must stretch to the limits our capacity to link the moment-by-moment quality of theater to the text. In large measure, this involves tracing potential energies as well as actions. Hamlet's attitudes toward time make a moment of inactivity early in the play radically different, for example, from a seemingly similar moment late in the play. The case of *Hamlet* is a particularly significant instance of a general principle: the dramatic text is uniquely time bound, and the refusal to reduce time to its spatial analogue offers new possibilities of reconciling the analysis of the dramatic text with the theatrical experience.[25]

Part II
Theatrical Text

3

Put Your Discourse into Some Frame:
Hamlet and the Uses of Wit

Hamlet's wit suggests qualities of mind that we can easily translate out of their tragic context. Hamlet is certainly the only one of Shakespeare's characters whom people consistently fantasize about inviting to dinner parties. They would prefer to forget that unpleasantness in Elsinore. But within the play this wit is not merely a decorative accessory. Our sense of reality suggests that it is not a sufficient weapon to depose the king of Denmark, but in the theater Hamlet's wit strongly informs our response to the words and gestures that constitute the play. Hamlet's wit initially makes us aware of his level of consciousness. When he later puts on his antic disposition, his wit provides opportunities for testing his environment, although at times we must question whether it helps or hinders his investigation. For most of the play, wit allows the audience distance from Hamlet's emotional turmoil, and when that distance is no longer possible, Hamlet's philosophical acceptance of his destiny makes empathy bearable. But for some time before this acceptance, an audience is left in a curious limbo in which wit concentrates ideas but cannot render them laughable. The disappearance of wit is ultimately as significant as its earlier presence.

Paradoxically, Freud's interpretation of wit is a strong argument against the standard Freudian reading of *Hamlet*.[1] Because the discourse of psychoanalysis makes extensive use of the myths of literature, it is not surprising to find fiction and psychoanalytic paradigm sharing a plot. But whereas the mythic plot is a summation for the psychoanalyst, it is a starting point for the artist. When myth becomes subject to the control of an individual artist, some degree of additional consciousness is exercised on the traditional plot. In general, the movement from epic literature to drama involving the same myth structure raises consciousness. For instance, a text that is to be acted, not narrated, must come to terms with violence. We observe this process in the classic Greek tragedies which constitute the most substantial body of dramatized myth in the Western tradition. In large measure we differentiate among the Greek tragedians by their ways of coming to terms with their mythic sources. For example, we observe that Aeschylus and Sophocles validate violence in ways which Euripedes avoids. Shakespeare's plays, like classic drama, come to terms with their narrative sources by raising the level of conscious exploration of the emotional consequences of mythic events. And the acting style of Shakespeare's theater certainly suggests that he is far more accountable than the Greeks for the moment-by-moment emotional reactions of his characters. The commentary provided by Hamlet's wit is one manifestation of a level of awareness which argues strongly against viewing him as dominated by unconscious motivations.

Freud hypothesizes that in joke-work (or wit-work) "a preconscious thought is given over for a moment to unconscious revision and the outcome of this is at once grasped by conscious perception."[2] Dream-work, on the other hand, is performed more consistently at the unconscious level and its outcome is not immediately accessible to conscious perception. The dreams that interest psychoanalysts are the product of barriers to conscious thought. But wit operates at a level where thought must be fairly open, though action might be barred. Most of the examples in Freud's study of wit, many of them Jewish humor, derive from situations where the joker is at a disadvantage in the power structure of society but acutely aware of where he stands. Similarly, the great witticisms in *Hamlet* occur early in the play before Hamlet is able to act but when he is contemplating most intensely his grievances against the established social order.

Hamlet's first utterance is a witticism and an aside. To Claudius's address, "my cousin Hamlet, and my son," he responds, "A little more than kin, and less than kind." In his first direct reply to Claudius, Hamlet finds himself "too much in the sun." Harping somewhat more crudely on a double meaning, he agrees with Gertrude that the death of kings is "common." The initial aside connects Hamlet's concern with the royal incest, his hostility to Claudius, and, plausibly if not certainly, his concern with who is king (a little more than kin). If this remark is indeed an aside (the decision to label it thus is modern), the no less hostile "too much in the sun" confronts the King directly. These initial witticisms are characteristic of how Hamlet's wit links the components of his grief and focuses his anger on his adversaries. Examining the genesis of wit in general, Freud ascribes the brevity of wit to an unconscious process by which condensation takes place, but his hypothesis demands a traffic between the conscious and unconscious (159–80). In terms of this Freudian model, Hamlet's quickness of wit suggests that his grievances are grouped in his mind and that he thinks about them as related. Moreover, his persistence argues that the outcome of his joke-work is quite clear to him.

This manifestation of a complex consciousness is significant because Hamlet's soliloquies tend to be single-minded, eloquent in their pursuit of a particular line of reasoning, but not responsive to the complexity of the events that precede them. Hamlet does not joke in soliloquy. Shakespeare seems to reserve the jocular tone in tragic soliloquy for such sociopaths as Edmund, Iago, and Richard III, whose joke is always on the world, not in it. Hamlet's wit is either contained within the dialogue or, if delivered as an aside, directly provoked by the dialogue. However, the source of wit in dialogue need not be pure confrontation. Hamlet's wit surfaces not only in encounters with his adversary Claudius but in his conversation with his friend Horatio. He ascribes to "thrift" his mother's hasty remarriage: "the funeral bak'd-meats / Did coldly furnish forth the marriage tables." Not only his moral outrage and his pain, but his sense of the epic vulgarity of Gertrude's behavior achieve a compressed expression, yet only the antecedent "thrift" anchors the denunciation in wit rather than lament. In a less concentrated form, we might find his disgust less attractive. (We do in general find it less attractive in the closet scene with his mother.) Hamlet's initial sallies of wit channel audience expectations. Before his deliberate adoption of the antic disposition, Hamlet's wit is established in the theater as a means of conveying complex ideas and within the play as a means of testing or provoking other people. (In the unique case of Horatio, "testing" becomes essentially confirmation of their shared perspective.)

The translation of the joke-work to the domain of the antic disposition is achieved largely by disconnecting Hamlet's premises for wit from the context of the dialogue. Instead of finding ironic dimensions within the pattern of conversation, he posits seeming absurdities (Polonius as fishmonger) and diverts the dialogue from its course into a forced exploration of his metaphor. The result resembles some of Pinter's effects: Hamlet's hostility is clear, but the context is opaque.

The techniques of Hamlet's wit change in response to the major shifts in the drama, but the varied devices are sufficiently interrelated to be viewed as a consistent component of his character. Hamlet's wit constitutes part of the menace he represents at the court, and in this he resembles his distant relative Amleth, hero of the Danish saga compiled by Saxo Grammaticus, which is the ultimate source of the story.[3] Though Amleth feigned imbecility rather than madness, he was also a riddler and a truth sayer. Early in his story, Amleth is laughed at for fire-hardening a collection of wooden hooks, which he calls javelins. Eventually he uses them to ensnare the King's guards. Amleth displays, in riddle form, the threat which he later manifests violently. Both Hamlet and his literary ancestor are approached by the murderous tyrants of their respective stories as puzzles that must be solved before they are killed. Like Hamlet, Amleth faces interrogation, sexual temptation, and espionage, before his life is directly threatened.

Outside fiction, the power invested in the words of the two heroes would not be plausible. In folklore, however, where riddle celebrates mind, its potency is considerable. In the theater, moreover, language dominates the stage. All other things being equal, the character whose words are most powerful is viewed as dominant in the territory represented by the stage space. This compensating characteristic of the theater preserves the potency of the folk figure whose weapon is words, though some of the energies that operate in folklore are defused by the customarily higher norms of rationality in the theater. Shakespeare's Hamlet appropriates a further word magic by bearing the name of his dead father. Hamlet's very survival makes Claudius's triumph palpably incomplete: Hamlet is dead; Hamlet lives.

The potentially murderous riddles of folklore are not the sole source of danger in wit. As a language of disguised meaning, wit evokes all the inherent ambivalence of the act of laughter. Freud describes the processes of wit as equivalent to those of dream: displacement and condensation.[4] For Lacan, as a post-Saussurean psychoanalyst, these processes may be described as metonymy and metaphor, which constitute, in his formulation, the primary processes of language itself. Poetic drama, such as *Hamlet*, intensifies these primary processes. In describing metaphor, Lacan defines a border between poetry and wit:

> We see, then, that metaphor occurs at the precise point at which sense emerges from non-sense, that is, at that frontier which, as Freud discovered, when crossed the other way produces the word that in French is *the* word *par excellence*, the word that is simply the signifier "*esprit*"; it is at this frontier that we realize that man defies his very destiny when he derides the signifier.[5]

At this frontier, and clearly with this import, stands Hamlet's speech, which crosses the border both ways, deriding the signifiers that buttress the power of Claudius but constantly refining sense from non-sense.

An ambiguity beyond that of language itself arises from the difficulty of determining the emotional tone underlying the dialogue. Fundamentally, of course, Hamlet's emotions are appropriate to the lugubrious circumstances that surround him. To joke, however, he must suspend or pretend to suspend these emotions in order to achieve the lack of feeling which, in Bergson's formulation, is a prerequisite condition for the laughable.[6] But how fully can a representation of Hamlet suspend such feelings? And how fully will an audience suspend its feelings in response to his signal? Moreover, Hamlet's joking takes place in an atmosphere that highlights human duplicity: he often deceives by pretending to pretend, by telling the truth when a lie is expected.[7] To use the terminology of Polonius, Hamlet's directness deceives, when indirectness is the norm. For the audience, what is joke within the plot may "read" as poetry, poetry as joke, because our perception of the border between sense and non-sense is different from, and more acute than, that of the characters who do not share Hamlet's consciousness of events.

Hamlet's determination to put on an antic disposition deliberately misaligns the expectations of his auditors within the play. This disposition pervades the scenes between the ghost's first appearance, which initiates the device, and the voyage to England. He is most broadly antic with Polonius, to whom he has proffered the red herring of a pretended love sickness over Ophelia. In the scene which establishes the characteristics of his madness, Hamlet makes Polonius the butt of his hostile humor, branding him fishmonger and quoting a satirist's derisive diatribe on old men. Yet, though he is the butt, Polonius is also in part an audience for Hamlet's wit, seeing that "Though this be madness, yet there's method in it."

For the audience proper, it is significant that Hamlet's mad wit
continues the metaphoric work of his sane wit. Hamlet's warnings about
Ophelia sustain the double meaning of "sun" that he established in his
first appearance.

> For if the sun breed maggots in a dead dog,
> being a good kissing carrion — Have you a daughter?
> . . . .
> Let her not walk i' th' sun. Conception is a
> blessing, but as your daughter may conceive, friend,
> look to't.
>
> (II.ii.181–82, 184–86)

The dramatic circumstances make a joke of what might be a kind of
prophetic poetry. Without the presupposition by Polonius of Hamlet's
madness and the inappropriate conversational context for language more
appropriate to a jeremiad, Hamlet's words would not provoke laughter.
The passage has not proved difficult to explicate, and an audience with
an ear for Shakespeare's reiterations of imagery will catch the echo of the
earlier "sun." The emotional ambivalence is perhaps less clear-cut.
Hamlet appears to warn against himself as sexual menace, but also
against Claudius (king as sun) as a breeder of corruption. Ophelia is thus
threatened by Hamlet but perceived as a parallel victim as well, like
Hamlet "in the sun," like Hamlet burdened by the flesh. There is a certain
two-facedness, perhaps, in arguing that Hamlet's wit must be perceived
as a manifestation of power when I have described its operation in terms
of a Freudian terminology that describes a kind of defense mechanism.
But the text itself is duplicitous in that Hamlet's consciousness is
imposed upon a saga which retains the essential elements of its narrative
virtually intact. Moreover, even the saga hero Amleth has a commitment
to truth which drives him to contrive elaborate scenarios in order to tell
the truth without being believed. Like Amleth, Hamlet risks himself,
anticipating the limitations of his adversaries in responding to his wit.

Not all of Hamlet's manic wit is sibylline in its obscurity. Hamlet
offers Polonius a typical fool's riddle as well: "for yourself, sir, shall
grow old as I am, if like a crab you could go backward." Polonius
perceives the surface rationality of the joke but does not see that he is
perceived as being in his second infancy, nor that Hamlet perceives
himself as being old in the burden of knowledge he bears. The effect of

Hamlet's humor again owes as much to his situation as to the structure of what he says. Normally, displacement, the diversion of thought from one train to another, serves as a protection (either psychological or social) to the joke teller. But Hamlet is a character in his own jokes, and the dialogue is displaced toward him rather than away from him. Nonsense, conventionally a delight in the free play of words, becomes for Hamlet a manner of expressing irreconcilable opposites. In the context of the play, Hamlet's jokes are not merely laden with double meaning, they are fraught with superfluous meaning. Hamlet offers not merely the simple irony of disparity between word and intention but the profound emotional ambivalence of hostility and sympathy, attack and instruction. The emotional neutrality of the joke allows this ambiguity to remain unresolved. And without emotion as a determining factor, words as signifiers are cut loose from determined meaning. More than ever, the language can be used, in Lacan's phrase, "in order to signify *something quite other* than what it says."[8]

The antic disposition establishes radical displacement as a conversational norm. Hamlet twists Polonius's mundane dialogue into an open expression of his own most intimate concerns.

> *Polonius.* Will you walk out of the air, my lord?
> *Hamlet.* Into my grave.

(II.ii.206–7)

And again:

> *Polonius.* My lord, I will take my leave of you.
> *Hamlet.* You cannot take from me any thing that I will not
> more willingly part withal — except my life, except my
> life, except my life.

(II.ii.213–17)

Hamlet's pregnant replies both sustain the tempo of his interaction with the court and enhance audience awareness of his proximity to despair. At the same time, manic wit distances the audience sufficiently from the emotional burden of empathy with Hamlet's suffering to allow an intellectual contemplation of the situation of the play.

Despite often being couched in terms suggesting philosophical objectivity, the soliloquies in *Hamlet* provide an audience little emotional distance from the protagonist: they incline to the progress of passion, not idea. Wit, however, sets the audience the task of making connections and exploring alternative meanings, a task which must be undertaken without the usual guidelines.[9] In conventional comedy, patterns are normally established which control the release of laughter. In those tragedies in which scenes of comic relief are carefully partitioned from the main plot, like the gatekeeper scene in *Macbeth*, an audience is usually directed to laugh at a low analogy to the main plot. Before the last act, there are few points in *Hamlet* at which we are unequivocally called upon to respond with laughter. The precondition of laughter — suspension of feeling — is never fully legitimized. Without comic structure to guarantee that laughter takes place within a social order, laughter becomes menacing. Far from providing an alternative to the tragic emotions, laughter intensifies them. Under these conditions, an audience will not respond uniformly. In a context in which laughter is not orchestrated, wit creates within the audience a variable emotional experience which alternates with the more determinate communal response to the soliloquies.[10]

The emotional indeterminacy of the play strongly inclines an audience to contemplate the indeterminacy of language. Hamlet's candor in dialogue is made possible not only by the assumption that he is mad but by a reluctance to know (or acknowledge) on the part of almost everyone in Elsinore. Their reluctance to know is remarkable in view of their devotion to espionage. Hamlet consistently assumes that, with the exception of what he says to Horatio, all his words will be reported or overheard. As a consequence of Hamlet's level of awareness, little dramatic irony is generated by a disparity between what he knows and what the audience knows. (Claudius's prayer scene is the exception.) Instead, the audience shares his ironic perception of how the gap between seeming and being in the state of Denmark deracinates language itself.

This persistent disruption of language increases the variability of the performed text, providing a high index of theatrality, a term Alter has defined as the potential for theatrical creativity by the performing artists. A high index of theatrality, which makes a play appealing to those who would stage it, suggests a strong risk of incoherence.[11] By the nature of *Hamlet*, however, the protagonist plays with signifiers; the actor's voice similarly at play does not distort the text. The very coherence of the text depends on the incoherence of the dialogue during the time when Hamlet maintains his antic disposition. Within the play, suspending the power of language suspends the language of power which has been usurped like power itself.[12]

Hamlet's encounter with Rosencrantz and Guildenstern demonstrates that the play's seemers derive no fundamental advantage from the deterioration of language. Hamlet's approach to them is a model of candor, their retreat to duplicity a paradigm of betrayal. If we look only at his language, it is difficult to see how they can call his conversation a crafty madness. His most sustained metaphor, "Denmark's a prison," is far more obvious than the buffoonery with which he disconcerts Polonius. Hamlet breaks off a line of banter about ambition with resignation — "I cannot reason" — rather than by distracting it into nonsense. His only foray into absurd language is his obscure, but compelling, "I am but mad north-north-west. When the wind is southerly I know a hawk from a hand-saw." A more attentive ear for an earlier statement would have set his betrayers on the right trail. "You are welcome; but my uncle-father and aunt-mother are deceiv'd." But the dramatic situation is subject to the assumption by Rosencrantz and Guildenstern that language is pretense. The refusal to know pervades their interrogation of Hamlet. They belabor a discussion of ambition as though forcing a card, but can do little with the strong hint concerning the incestuous marriage. Hamlet's initial efforts with them are an attempt to educate "the indifferent children of the earth." His final effort, their death warrant, mythologizes their ignorance in the face of words.

Hamlet's wit serves often to add dimensions of meaning to scenarios devised by others. He is, however, sufficiently aggressive either to refuse frameworks which do not suit his purposes or to substitute his own. In situations where he is involved in clear conflicts, Hamlet disrupts the dialogue. He uses the mental momentum of his adversaries to provoke them to verbal pratfalls. On these occasions, he characteristically denies the illocutionary force of their statements. This manner of warding off his opponents serves not to avoid issues but to deny their power over him.[13] The messengers who seek him after the Mousetrap play are subjected to this radical disruption of their logic. The King, says Guildenstern, "Is in his retirement marvellous distemp'red." "With drink, sir?" asks Hamlet. Guildenstern is soon forced to plead that Hamlet cease his joking: "Good my lord, put your discourse into some frame, and start not so wildly from my affair." But, as Hamlet well knows, whoever controls the framework of discourse controls the power of the signifiers.

In defining his own framework, Hamlet initiates comic processes that, unlike those of comedy proper, tend to suspend or bracket the vices of the characters involved rather than to display them in action. Henri Bergson's familiar theory of laughter contends that the human becomes laughable through a descent in which we see "the body taking precedence of the soul."[14] For the various tools of Claudius, this descent is defined by their surrender of their moral responsibility to the will of the crown. But Hamlet makes puppets of these characters in simple physical ways, as if by analogy to instruct them in their more profound failings. He seems not to discover and expose the actual crimes of the King's henchmen in the manner of the eiron, but to intuit their flaws and to toy with their fundamental weakness.[15]

Hamlet's most elaborate joke with Rosencrantz and Guildenstern is essentially homiletic. In response to successive requests that he play the recorder, Guildenstern asserts four times that he cannot play. At last Hamlet proffers instructions: "It is as easy as lying. Govern these vent-ages with your fingers and thumbs." Another denial of skill precedes the lesson that concludes the prank.

> Why, look you now, how unworthy a thing
> you make of me! You would play upon me, you would
> seem to know my stops, you would pluck out the
> heart of my mystery, you would sound me from my
> lowest note to the top of my compass; and there is
> much music, excellent voice, in this little organ, yet
> cannot you make it speak. 'S blood, do you think I am
> easier to be play'd on than a pipe? Call me what
> instrument you will, though you fret me, yet you
> cannot play upon me.

(III.ii.363–72)

Trapped in a mechanical reaction, Guildenstern ends up the butt of a practical joke that also allows Hamlet a verbal assertion of his own human freedom. The situation is aptly described by Bergson's model of the laughable, the human subjected to a "mechanical inelasticity."[16] Hamlet is able to demonstrate to the King's instrument that he is not himself an instrument, an inanimate device governed by physical laws. Simultaneously, he asserts his independence from the exclusively human mechanism of language: "Call me what instrument you will ... you cannot play upon me."

Using the mechanical responses of the court instruments to fret them, Hamlet elaborates for the audience the distinction between human choice and mechanical behavior. Polonius, the messenger who succeeds Rosencrantz and Guildenstern in this scene, is led to agree that a cloud on the horizon is like a camel, a weasel, a whale, whatever Hamlet names it. Assuming that his assent must be acted, Polonius must look, perceive the pattern, and agree — three times. The simple repetition of the request that Guildenstern play is thus succeeded by an actual playing upon Polonius that extends the metaphor of man as instrument from dialogue to dramatic enactment.

In the cases I have examined thus far, Hamlet is in control, taunting the King or demonstrating, often offhandedly, the intellectual and moral vacuity of the underlings who mean to manipulate him. But not all of Hamlet's joking manifests so clear a control of mind over emotion. At several moments of crisis within the play, Hamlet jokes grotesquely, violating our expectations of respect for the dead and taxing even the Elizabethan sense of acceptable sexual innuendo. The contemplation of the horrible seems to urge Hamlet to a crude humor that reflects in his language the larger breakdown in order, a breakdown that would seem to make verbal propriety absurd. The emotional excitement provoked by the ghost's appearance in Act I leads Hamlet to the shocking jocularity of comparing him to a mole as the voice moves beneath the stage. Hamlet's banter with "truepenny" in the cellarage suggests some insight into his abuse of the other family — Polonius, Ophelia, and Laertes. Hamlet is moved to answer shock with shock without evaluating his response. Provoked by their proximity to his distress, Hamlet cannot acknowledge that the family of Polonius occupies a middle ground: they act as servants of the crown, but, until Laertes is provoked by the death of Polonius and the madness of Ophelia, they are innocent of malice.

Within the play, Hamlet could never be termed successful as a joker. He is rarely aligned with his wit in the normal manner. Aloofness and anguish alternate in him. In some instances, he deploys jokes to assert his intellectual power. In others, he becomes entangled in the matter of his jokes, creating the verbal structures of wit without an appropriate emotional stance. Hamlet demonstrates his mastery in manipulating words as signifiers but remains helpless to establish value because the words that buttress power — father, mother, king, marriage — are the very words needed to convey value.[17]

Hamlet's shock at his father's death and mother's remarriage results in a twofold revulsion for the body: a contempt for sexuality and an acute awareness of bodily decay. His contempt for sexuality, which contaminates but does not diminish his own sexual response, becomes the source of his coarse ribaldry. When the words that denote family relations have been devalued, all references to sexuality are obscene. Equally obscene are references to death. Denied the proper words and rituals of human mourning, Hamlet must express his reaction to his father's death improperly or not at all. His preoccupation with decay fuels the gallows humor that accompanies the first appearance of the ghost, the moment when he contemplates his father's death, and, most pointedly, the death of Polonius. When the sea voyage has put space and time between Hamlet and the first eruption of violence within the play, humor is no longer a necessary vehicle for him to express his relationship to the flesh. In the graveyard scene of Act V, he continues to contemplate the decay of the body, but his rumination is not dominated by gallows humor. Rather, it is characterized by a sadness that acknowledges grief rather than distances it. Subsequently, Hamlet is able to speak of having loved Ophelia, in particular of having loved her as a brother could not.

At the core of Hamlet's disillusionment is his vivid conception of husband and wife as becoming one flesh in a bond stronger than blood kinship. Through this perception of marriage, which the Christian wedding ceremony enjoins, Gertrude's incest is not merely legally forbidden but palpably loathsome. Hamlet's reference to the disruption of kinship by his uncle-father and aunt-mother peaks in intensity in the manic moment before he is sent to England, when he bids farewell to Claudius:

> My mother: father and mother is man and
> wife, man and wife is one flesh — so, my mother.
>
> (IV.iii.51–52)

A final image of the marriage bond emerges in the duel scene when Hamlet forces Claudius to drink the poisoned wine.

> Here, thou incestious, murd'rous, damned Dane,
> Drink off this potion! Is thy union here?
> Follow my mother!
>
> (V.ii.325–27)

The "union" is, of course, both the pearl that contained the poison and Claudius's marriage to Gertrude.

Hamlet's preoccupation with the terms of the marriage vow fuels the Freudian argument that Hamlet's dilemma is essentially Oedipal, but *Hamlet* is not the only play in the Shakespearean canon to invoke the language of the wedding ceremony. *Lear* similarly plays with the idea that marriage dissolves boundaries. At Edmund's death, he, Goneril, and Regan "marry in an instant." Earlier in *Lear*, Albany bids that Regan woo him because his wife is contracted to Edmund. He implies that for Regan to affix herself to the open end of a chain of contracts that links Albany, Goneril, and Edmund is equivalent to her marrying Edmund because the marriage bond creates a transitivity of relationship. By a similar line of reasoning, Hamlet's flesh is sullied by its bond to Claudius through Gertrude. In *Hamlet*, as in *Lear*, commentary on the violation of the qualities of marriage most congruent with its Christian purpose emerges in grim jokes rather than in the longer contemplative passages. In general, we must be wary of taking the long speeches as definitive summations of what is happening in Shakespeare's tragedies.

By Gertrude's remarriage, the words woman, wife, and mother are devalued, and Ophelia, the woman Hamlet would have made wife and mother, becomes instead a surrogate for his revulsion. Although Ophelia's obedience to her father's command offends Hamlet at a time when he feels no transgression to be venial, it is clear that he has no words left to describe benevolently the relation of man and woman. His tendency to generalize the individual offense is common enough among Shakespeare's tragic heroes. The behavior of Lear's daughters leads him to denounce marriage: he will have "copulation thrive." Cressida's infidelity provokes Troilus's cry, "Let it not be believ'd for womanhood," and Ulysses' rejoinder, "What hath she done, Prince, that can soil our mothers?" Characteristically in Shakespeare, any primary breakdown of human relationships devalues all the signifiers of family relationship. To an audience, however, Ophelia's personal offense seems comparatively slight. If she is used by the court to stalk Hamlet, he seems no less willing to use her as a diversion in the Mousetrap scene. A critic or an audience must find a way to reconcile Hamlet's behavior with his later claim to have loved her. Whatever personal feeling he has for her must emerge in the tone of scenes in which she figures primarily as a signifier.[18]

Hamlet's behavior toward Ophelia in the nunnery scene reveals much about his emotional stance toward sexuality. Though it does not make use of sexual humor, the scene is inextricable from this discussion because it is the conceptual complement of his bawdy behavior during the Mousetrap play. The scene is primarily a denunciation of the capacity of marriage to breed. Incidentally, but only incidentally, Hamlet rails on women with the commonplaces of the satirist. The keystone of the dialogue is Hamlet's discourse upon his own sinfulness, which is merely the sinfulness of being human.

> Get thee to a nunn'ry, why wouldst thou
> be a breeder of sinners? I am myself indifferent honest,
> but yet I could accuse me of such things that it were
> better my mother had not borne me: I am very proud,
> revengeful, ambitious, with more offenses at my beck
> than I have thoughts to put them in, imagination to
> give them shape, or time to act them in. What should
> such fellows as I do crawling between earth and
> heaven? We are arrant knaves, believe none of us. Go
> thy ways to a nunn'ry.
>
> (III.i.120–29)

If we assume reasonable consistency of tone, it is unlikely that "nunn'ry" is spoken so mockingly as to force its slang meaning, brothel. Hamlet tends to vilify sexuality in intense and sustained passages, not in isolated allusions. Nor does Ophelia seem to respond to a threatening onslaught, either verbal or physical. She voices concern at his loss of wits, not fear for her own safety. The battering to which modern stage practice often condemns her seems to me to conflate Hamlet's behavior here with his behavior both at the Mousetrap play and in his mother's closet. In context, Hamlet extends his sense of the burden of existence, the issue contemplated in the "To be or not to be" soliloquy that directly precedes the scene. Whatever affection Hamlet will express for a living Ophelia must find an outlet in the elegiac tone of what must be for both of them a farewell to the possibility of happiness.

At the Mousetrap play, Hamlet's tone is quite different. Engaged in an act of provocation against the King, he is concerned with sexuality as a motive to crime, but not with the danger of procreation as a source of more sinners. The purpose of Hamlet's coarse sexual humor seems overdetermined. It has in part the most common of motives — an excess of sexual energy denied its natural outlet. Hamlet's "It would cost you a groaning to take off mine edge" is not entirely diversion. But Hamlet's words in the scene reverberate with other meanings throughout the play. The violent undercurrent of the metaphor is not lost on an audience that knows that Hamlet's keen edge will cost Claudius a groaning. In the absence of distinct signals that the borders of what we will accept as joking have been crossed, we are inclined to allow Hamlet considerable scope without withdrawing our sympathy.

Because the Mousetrap play provides a focal point for the scene, Hamlet's comments need not create a structure; consequently, they are wide ranging. Hamlet takes Ophelia's remark on his merriment as an occasion to comment on his mother's demeanor.

> O God, your only jig-maker. What should a
> man do but be merry, for look you how cheerfully my
> mother looks, and my father died within 's two hours.
>
> (III.ii.125–27)

He diverts Ophelia's questions about the dumb show into a bawdy joke about showing pregnancy: "Be not you asham'd to show, he'll not shame to tell you what it means." Hamlet has not forgotten his deeper concerns. Ophelia's comment on the aesthetic and moral qualities of a remark that she finds "still better, and worse" allows his reply, "So you mistake your husbands." The response adds to the accumulating store still another phrase that characterizes the Christian marriage ceremony (to take each other for better or worse).

Yet the main line of this conversation is a kind of bitter bawdry. How does the play guide audience response to such sexual humor, or at least rough hew that response? Hamlet's verbal preoccupation with lying between maid's legs, country matters, groaning, showing, and sexual keenness reflects an uncharacteristically low vein of humor in him. But an audience is accustomed at this point to laughing at Hamlet's jokes and puns. The momentum of this habit is greater in the theater than in the study, and it carries easily through the Mousetrap scene. Because this scene focuses on the manifestation of Claudius's guilt, our attitude toward Hamlet is not radically altered by his language. Nor does Ophelia seem perturbed. She allows him to lie at her feet with his head in her lap, comments (with appropriate moral disclaimers) on the quickness of his wit, and has it in her power to divert or interrupt the conversation at will. Hamlet's capacity for coarseness with Ophelia, however, lays the groundwork for his sexual vituperation in the scene in Gertrude's closet, and for his degradation of the dead Polonius.

The theatrical momentum of Hamlet's wit encounters a major barrier when he kills Polonius. As Hamlet jokes about this death, our impulse to laugh conflicts with our sympathy for Polonius. Hamlet's gallows humor begins to grate. The situation differs from the ghost scene on the battlements, where we sympathize with his distress, in that Hamlet causes the death of Polonius and takes little time to acknowledge responsibility for what he has done. Hamlet's point of view loses much of its privilege over the stretch of time when the audience sees him kill Polonius, precipitate Ophelia's insanity, and abuse Laertes at Ophelia's grave site. Until the death of Polonius, the audience enjoys sharing Hamlet's privileged knowledge of the ghost's revelations. When Hamlet's wit manifests his control of the complexities in which he is entangled, the audience laughs, delighted with his condensation of the issues of the play. But killing Polonius, the wrong man, is the antithesis of control. The limited possibility of laughter at Hamlet's mockery of Polonius's death depends on whatever pleasure is derived from the release of restraints surrounding our attitude toward the dead, given the underlying awareness of the audience that the death is merely a stage death. Such laughter has its place in the spectrum of comedy, but an audience cannot so suddenly distance itself from the seriousness of death when the drama, in the main, encourages precisely the opposite attitude.

A principle has begun to emerge: that of determining the disposition of the audience toward Hamlet's jokes by ascertaining the focus of the dramatic context. In III.iv, this context is particularly complex: the dying Polonius is clearly upstaged by both Hamlet's confrontation of his mother and the ghostly visitation. The dominant mechanism of Hamlet's gallows humor is to ignore the difference between a live and a dead Polonius. But death, in this scene, is not simply defined. Hamlet acts as if the marriage of his parents is not terminated by death. His dead father continues to play an active role in Hamlet's relationship with his mother, not merely reciting the past but perceiving her "warring soul" in the present. Hamlet himself is, as always, more than half envious of death. These conditions moderate, though they do not eliminate, our adverse

reaction to Hamlet's savagery. His remarks to the dead Polonius bracket
his confrontation of the Queen. His initial reaction is casually brutal.

> Thou wretched, rash, intruding fool, farewell!
> I took thee for thy better. Take thy fortune;
> Thou find'st to be too busy is some danger.
>
> (III.iv.31–33)

After Hamlet's confrontation with his mother, Polonius is perceived
more clearly as a body ("the guts"). A joke is derived from the verbal
image of Polonius as doer ("This man shall set me packing") and the
physical presence of the body as a material burden.

> This man shall set me packing;
> I'll lug the guts into the neighbor room.
> Mother, good night indeed. This counsellor
> Is now most still, most secret, and most grave,
> Who was in life a foolish prating knave.
>
> (III.iv.211–15)

Within the scene, Hamlet's repentance for the death of Polonius is
inappropriately succinct. He shows no awareness, for example, that the
death will affect Ophelia and Laertes.

> For this same lord,
> I do repent; but heaven hath pleas'd it so
> To punish me with this, and this with me,
> That I must be their scourge and minister.
> I will bestow him, and will answer well
> The death I gave him.
>
> (III.iv.172–77)

After the death of Polonius, we remain somewhat estranged from
Hamlet even when his joking resumes some of its former purposes.
When the presence of the King reestablishes a legitimate object for
Hamlet's hostility, he only partially regains our sympathy. Hamlet's
jocular hesitation to reveal where he has hidden the body allows him
simultaneously to contemplate mortality and to threaten the King.
Polonius is "at supper ..."

> Not where he eats, but where 'a is eaten; a
> certain convocation of politic worms are e'en at
> him. Your worm is your only emperor for diet: we
> fat all creatures else to fat us, and we fat ourselves for
> maggots; your fat king and your lean beggar is but var-
> iable service, two dishes, but to one table — that's the
> end.
>
> (IV.iii.19–25)

When Hamlet reveals where he has hidden Polonius, the jest produced by ignoring the difference between body and soul draws attention to the distinction between the two. He informs Claudius that Polonius is ...

> In heaven, send thither to see; if your
> messenger find him not there, seek him i' th' other
> place yourself. But if indeed you find him not
> within this month, you shall nose him as you go up the
> stairs into the lobby.
>
> (IV.iii.33–37)

Although the device of condensation still operates in these passages, and we are thus efficiently kept in touch with a number of the play's concerns, Hamlet has declined from effectively expressing the moral plight of Denmark to attempting to extricate meaning from his own ineffective action. Before we can completely share Hamlet's perspective once again, the gallows humor surrounding the death of Polonius must be redeemed, not by words alone but by the display of human sympathies in the graveyard scene.

The themes provoked by the death of Polonius reemerge in the graveyard. But there Hamlet is no longer the creator of jokes. The grave digger, accustomed to the presence of death, is the joker, and Hamlet, with Horatio, the audience. Disconnected as these jokes are from the particulars of the plot, they tend to allay our sense of horror. Before Hamlet and Horatio arrive, the grave digger and his assistant exchange commonplace jokes. Their riddle about who builds best provokes two contending answers: the gallows maker and the grave maker. They riddle about Adam — a fellow digger, the first to bear arms. But before this trivial array of witticisms, their humor reduces the question of Ophelia's Christian burial to basic principles.

Is she to be buried in Christian burial when
she willfully seeks her own salvation?

. . . .

How can that be, unless she drowned herself in her own defense?

(V.i.1–2, 6–7)

They protest the privilege of the nobility in naive terms: "And the more pity that great folk should have count'nance in this world to drown or hang themselves, more than their even-Christen." The childlike quality of their humor renders it inoffensive.

Surprisingly, given the macabre humor of Hamlet's last previous appearance in the play, he finds the singing of the grave maker anomalous: "Has this fellow no feeling of his business?" The most obvious new element Hamlet brings to the scene is feeling for the dead. His concerns with the decay of the flesh are much the same as they were earlier. He perceives the paradox of ambition come to nothing when worms and maggots consume the flesh, but his own "bones ache" to think of how the bones are knocked about. Hamlet bandies a few equivocations with the grave digger about whether the man lies in the grave he stands in, but he is no longer generating emotional distance for himself within the play, nor is emotional distance generated in the theater for the audience. Hamlet acknowledges the loss involved in death in his well-known lament for Yorick, the clown. Hamlet peoples the cemetery with imaginary lives and summons the past from memory. His feeling for Yorick signals the death of a particular kind of humor. Hamlet addresses the skull of Yorick:

Now get you
to my lady's chamber, and tell her, let her paint an
inch thick, to this favor she must come; make her
laugh at that.

(V.i.192–95)

In the interim between this scene and his death, Hamlet ceases to laugh at the things that wound him most deeply.

Hamlet's use of wit provides an audience with a barometer of his capacity to feel. What we admire first as an ability to control emotion, the distancing effect of humor, we come to lament as an inability to feel emotion properly. When the dying begins, wit is no longer perceived as potential energy, a waiting power in Hamlet. The change is reflected in our uneasiness in laughing at his gallows humor. The graveyard scene allows us laughter at death — the grave makers are not expected to exercise their craft feelingly — but signals clearly that Hamlet's need to crystallize unresolved tension into wit and to distance the most painful circumstances of his life has passed. In the final analysis, Hamlet's wit is not a decorative accessory to the action of the play but a vital part of our perception of his loss of touch with the world and subsequent return to it.

For many, the disappearance of the kind of wit that categorizes the first four acts of *Hamlet* is pure loss, an almost Brechtian discontinuity in Hamlet's character.[19] Certainly much of what we value in the play is the assault on language that Hamlet undertakes when the signifiers have lost their meaning because the institutions of marriage and government have been undermined. After Hamlet's return from the sea, he is no longer "deriding the signifier." Rather, he seems to defend established words and customs against distortion, equivocation, and excess. In effect, Hamlet no longer blames language for the disruption of order.

Hamlet's confrontation with Laertes is more understandable if we are aware of his new role as defender of the signifier. He "reads" correctly that the "maimed rites" signify suicide. In the midst of his grotesque intrusion on Laertes' grief, Hamlet's concern with language is easily overlooked.

> What is he whose grief
> Bears such an emphasis, whose phrase of sorrow
> Conjures the wand'ring stars and makes them stand
> Like wonder-wounded hearers? This is I,
> Hamlet the Dane!
>
> (V.i.254–58)

His commentary on Laertes' language accompanies his announcement of himself by name, the name that was his father's and that, when coupled with the name of his country, announces his right to kingship. He never subsequently refers to Claudius as father, and Hamlet Senior ("my King") is clearly not conflated with the public figure in power ("the King"). When Hamlet dies, he will leave Horatio to tell his story and save him from a "wounded name." When the key signifiers are restored, words once again have meaning.[20]

Hamlet's account to Horatio of the "changeling" commission that sends Rosencrantz and Guildenstern to death suggests his control over the process of signification. His power to impose his own message depends first on his penmanship, the ability to write signs that others can read.

> I once did hold it, as our statists do,
> A baseness to write fair, and labor'd much
> How to forget that learning, but, sir, now
> It did me yeman's service.
>
> (V.ii.33–36)

Hamlet's message is sealed with a sign of kingship over which he has power: his father's signet ring.

When signifiers no longer afflict Hamlet, he defends words against the abuse of courtiers like Osric for whom to "signify" is to "speak sellingly." We are astonished to see Hamlet, whose style of speech in dialogue has been characterized by intense condensation, parody the courtier's euphuism in praising Laertes.

> Sir, his definement suffers no perdition in
> you, though I know to divide him inventorially
> would dozy th' arithmetic of memory, and yet but
> yaw neither in respect of his quick sail; but in
> the verity of extolment, I take him to be a soul of
> great article, and his infusion of such dearth and rare-
> ness as, to make true diction of him, his semblable is
> his mirror, and who else would trace him, his um-
> brage, nothing more.
>
> (V.ii.112–20)

When he so chooses, Hamlet plays "the tune of the time" more adeptly than the timeserver Osric, but he advocates simplicity of language.[21]

Hamlet's return to a belief in language is a concrete part of his faith in the world — a "harsh world," but not a world without value. In the end, it matters to him what reputation he leaves in the world and who becomes king of Denmark. Hamlet's elaborate attack on words can ultimately be seen to have resulted from the disruption of his intense desire to believe in words. His final advocacy of language is the logical outcome of his struggle against a usurpation of power that includes a usurpation of the power of the signifier.

4
About, My Brains!
Hamlet's Soliloquies

In soliloquy we are most acutely aware of the actor as actor, as performer in relationship to an audience. Although in part the convention suggests a character talking to himself, or herself, who remains within the drama, the speaker is nonetheless circumstantially addressing a theater audience. Consequently, the soliloquy is likely to be characterized by many of the gestures of public speech, both physical and rhetorical. The substance of the address usually bears out the paramount importance of the audience, as it does, for example, in the explanation of motivations that characterizes so many soliloquies. A soliloquy makes us privileged spectators of what is to follow, much as perspective makes us privileged spectators of Renaissance painting. Yet the process by which we acquire this privilege continues to define the fictional character enmeshed in the drama that is being enacted. To be aware of ourselves as audience, as we are when we are directly addressed, is to be aware not only of our privileged perspective (an awareness that disengages us) but also of our process of synthesis (an awareness that reengages us).

Our reception of a soliloquy involves constituting into a whole a character's abstracted self-representation in soliloquy together with what we observe of the character within the action of the play — that is, his/her self-representation within the society defined by the play. In order to perform this synthesis, we judge (at least implicitly) the relationship of the use of soliloquy in a particular play to the play's other ways of presenting. For example, Macbeth in soliloquy reveals depths of consciousness that his actions do not reflect. Iago lures the audience

91

through laughter into mock complicity with actions we subsequently loathe. Prince Hal reveals his awareness of the pattern of the prodigal's return that will follow in *Henry IV, Part 1*, and he is consequently distanced from his own "holiday." In Shakespeare, the relationship of soliloquy to dialogue is complex and variable, but it characteristically creates a tension between a character and his behavior or provides an audience with new codes to interpret that behavior.

Maurice Charney has argued that the text of *Hamlet* suggests a practice in which soliloquies, much like asides, did little to interrupt the flow of stage action. He is most convincing in arguing the case for Claudius and Polonius, but he also observes that Hamlet's soliloquies do not demand an empty stage. Notably, "To be or not to be" takes place while Claudius and Polonius are hidden behind an arras, and a later soliloquy may even be viewed as embedded in Claudius's prayer soliloquy.[1] Charney's observations caution us against an excessively disjointed analysis of the play's components. But, despite the encroachment of the play's action on Hamlet's soliloquies, they establish a sustained and intimate relationship with the audience, which Ralph Berry calls an "extended ingratiation."[2] I am not as convinced as is Berry that "charm" is essential, but I would agree that more than any other role in Shakespeare, that of Hamlet requires a star, with all the diversion of our attention from the narrative that the star-audience relationship entails. Casting a star in the role (and the practice is certainly not new) will tend to isolate soliloquy, that is, to highlight the moments when the audience has the star "all to itself."

The most famous of Hamlet's soliloquies, those that have tended both to become set pieces and to dominate critical discussion, differ radically from his speech in dialogue. Whereas his conversation normally reflects the doubleness of meaning characteristic of wit, his soliloquies are characteristically single-minded expressions of emotion. Rather than presenting the full range of Hamlet's response to his dilemma, they tend to express moods of grief, despair, self-reproach, even malice, and to do so at times when immediately preceding events may not seem to justify the emotional response. Moreover, a given soliloquy may foreground a rhetorical style or philosophical methodology that is not elsewhere characteristic of the protagonist even in the other soliloquies. Though soliloquy isolates and highlights aspects of Hamlet's experience, it has no special privilege in representing that experience. The use of soliloquy seems to complement the use of wit in the dialogue; both are important constituents of the first part of the play. Soliloquy disappears (and wit is severely curtailed) after Hamlet's sea voyage. His final perceptions of his experience are expressed to Horatio in a manner quite different from that of his earlier confidences. In Act V, Hamlet can be candid without the defense mechanism of wit that distances him from Horatio earlier in the play. Rather than bring philosophical stances to bear on "things in heaven and earth" that are beyond them, he can adopt a philosophy that represents his perspective.

The key to the relationship of Hamlet's soliloquies to his wit is that the two manners of presentation constitute the poles of emotional distance. Wit may reflect strong emotions, but it does not directly express them. If wit reflects pain, it does so through the auditor's intellectual awareness that the constructs of wit produce laughter in circumstances where the underlying experience is painful. Hamlet's manic wit, intensified by the pretense of madness, allows him an ample opportunity to express the cause of his discontent, but only a limited opportunity to express its effect on him. In particular, he cannot discuss in public his reaction to the burden of revenge. And given the scope of the conspiracy against him, his alternatives are to discuss this burden with Horatio or with himself.

Viewed as an active agent in the play, Horatio would be absurd. He spends months watching events that extinguish the royal line of Denmark and bring a foreign power to the throne, and neither acts nor suggests action. Subsequently, he offers to commit suicide. Yet this description hardly represents his function in the play or our reaction to him. Horatio is more easily described as a stage device than as a character. As a confidant, he is a vital channel of information, becoming privy to Hamlet's plans for the Mousetrap play, receiving a letter that informs us of Hamlet's encounter with the pirates, and ultimately sharing Hamlet's final thoughts on the meaning of his life. Paradoxically, Hamlet feels completely isolated yet enjoys what constitutes a model of faithful friendship. We are not confused by the contradiction because our experience is ordered by the play. Hamlet's sense of isolation is conveyed through the predominance of soliloquy early in the play; his later sense of a providential Nature is conveyed through the more prominent companionship of Horatio late in the play. But even so trusted a friend as Horatio is initially allowed to view only a rationalized self-image of Hamlet.

Until Hamlet is more fully reconciled to himself, he shares his doubts with no one, and his expression of doubt is relegated to soliloquy. Only in soliloquy is Hamlet's relationship to his father (his absent father, his dead father, his father's ghost) seen as problematic. In dialogue, his immediate objectives are determined by those who are present. The presence of Rosencrantz and Guildenstern, for example, provokes Hamlet to evaluate their honesty or to convey to the King that he is not deceived. Even the appearances of the ghost, which in the abstract might seem to afford an opportunity for dialogue, do little to explore the relations of Hamlet to his father. The ghostly presence is a corporeal absence, and, although there are no rules for such matters, ghostly visitations are more conducive to messages than to dialogue. Nor is it easy for other dialogue within the play to explore the implications of the ghost's visit. Only the audience, privy to what the ghost says (in his first revelation and in his later exhortation), is attuned to the power of this external force. Characters other than Hamlet within the play are not. We will never be fully satisfied with the relation of the soliloquies to the scenes that surround them if we expect to regard them as tightly linked to a sequence of events. They occur in rhythmic alternation with the dialogue to present those aspects of Hamlet's experience that the dialogue cannot, not because of any inherent limitations of dialogue, but because dialogue embeds a character within a social fabric that Hamlet is denied. Had the choice been made to expand Horatio's already extensive role as trusted friend, he would approach being Hamlet's coconspirator in a plot against the crown. Such a choice would make Hamlet a more public figure and *Hamlet* a more political play.

While Hamlet is assimilating the events at Elsinore, roughly until the sea voyage, his actions are largely reflected in dialogue, his reactions in soliloquy. The Hamlet who has become a component of Western culture rather than a character in Shakespeare's play has been heavily biased toward the long speeches (and hence largely toward the soliloquies) in which we presumably find what Hamlet is "like" independent of what he does. This creature, a Hamlet doppelganger who has been almost as influential as Shakespeare's Hamlet, is pathologically incapable of action. The soliloquies, deprived of their counterbalance, weigh too heavily in the scales. Out of the context of the actions that surround them, the soliloquies do not in their natural order constitute a clear philosophical or psychological pattern. The most important of the soliloquies are generalized reactions to Hamlet's situation. Two suggest despair; two are gestures of self-reproach. The remaining three are soliloquies of immediate reaction, emotionally continuous with the events that precede them: Hamlet reacts to the ghost, to the Mousetrap play, and to the opportunity to kill Claudius. Within these groups, the speeches suggest some progression, but the sense of thematic reiteration is equally strong.

Hamlet's two soliloquies of despair have perplexed critics primarily because they are separated by the revelations of the ghost but seem similar in attitude. To the Freudian school this suggests that Hamlet's own feeling of guilt is the primary determinant of his behavior. The continuity of Hamlet's aversion to Claudius and Gertrude may even be construed as suggesting that the ghost is a manifestation of Hamlet's reaction to his father's death and mother's remarriage, not an independent agent. But though the two speeches emanate from a common ground of melancholy, their philosophical and rhetorical methodologies are strikingly different.

The first soliloquy, "O that this too too sallied flesh would melt," (I.ii.129–59) poses a critical puzzle. It is the only soliloquy to precede the ghost's revelation, yet in it Hamlet is as characteristically isolated as anywhere in the play.

> O that this too too sallied flesh would melt,
> Thaw and resolve itself into a dew!
> Or that the Everlasting had not fix'd
> His canon 'gainst self-slaughter! O God, God,
> How weary, stale, flat, and unprofitable
> Seem to me all the uses of this world!
>
> (I.ii.129–34)

Much more explicitly related to his personal grievance than the later "To be or not to be," the soliloquy gives vent to what cannot enter the dialogue if Hamlet indeed will hold his tongue. As is characteristic of a first soliloquy, the speech acquaints us with the significance of a situation, the stance of a character in that situation, and his sense of what will ensue, but what is unusual is that Hamlet intuits what is to come but does not suggest that he will precipitate events.

The soliloquy is also remarkable in its implicit adherence to norms of value. Even the impulse to "self-slaughter," which evokes for the reader or audience familiar with the play the subsequent "To be or not to be," is subordinated to God's canon. Moreover, the impulse to suicide is only an alternative to Hamlet's first desire, a distillation of sorts that would transform the "sallied flesh" into pure dew. Despite this impulse to achieve an absolute transformation, Hamlet focuses a remarkable proportion of his attention on social codes of propriety. The haste of his mother's remarriage receives more lengthy attention, both in this soliloquy and subsequently in the play, than his concern that the marriage between a widow and her late husband's brother is, at least technically, incestuous. (Despite the marital difficulties of Henry VIII that focused attention on this issue for a Tudor audience, it is doubtful that this form of incest has ever had the power to evoke in an audience the horror that consanguineous incest evokes.)

The central source of value in the soliloquy is natural law. Whereas Claudius had turned to nature to escape social order, arguing that nature's theme is death of fathers, Hamlet sees the beast as bedrock, providing a minimum standard of behavior that human reason should exceed. Hamlet's lament over his mother's remarriage is a mixture of appeals to propriety and nature. There seems an implicit reproach in his description of both Gertrude's attachment to her husband, "as if increase of appetite had grown by what it fed on," and her grief, "like Niobe, all tears." (We might anticipate Hamlet's reaction to Laertes' excesses at Ophelia's grave.) Claudius is seen as Hamlet Senior's inferior in the order of nature, admittedly a mythologized nature, a satyr to Hamlet's Hyperion. Even the argument that Gertrude's shoes outlasted her grief appeals to an order in which spirit should outlast mutable matter. Hamlet's rejection of the world as an unweeded garden epitomizes the principles of his reasoning in this soliloquy. The image is quite conventional and public. In the garden, human reason combines harmoniously with nature; the unweeded garden suggests the abdication of reason from a contract with nature.

Within its limits, Hamlet's reasoning in the soliloquy is unimpeachable. His allusions and images for the most part suggest a continued allegiance to classical rhetoric. Even his conclusion — "It is not nor it cannot come to good, / But break my heart for I must hold my tongue" — reflects both an implicit faith that wrongdoing cannot survive and a continued deference to his mother, whose wishes he has just promised to obey. His first impulse is to preserve social order, however much he may disapprove of its most recent restructuring. Hamlet's stance is remarkably conservative: human behavior, even of the most appalling kind, does not suggest to him that values are themselves invalidated. But even more conservative than his conclusions is his philosophical methodology, which is essentially descriptive rather than exploratory. Neither the appeal to canon law nor the appeal to an already codified natural law offers a possibility of discovering an unknown. From the beginning, the soliloquy searches for an orderly description of the crisis rather than a resolution.

Hamlet's second speech of despair, "To be or not to be" (III.i.55–87), is less closely linked to the immediate chain of events and is more abstractly philosophical, so much so that reading the speech has become a kind of scholarly cottage industry. Our reception of the speech is complicated not only by its abstract relationship to the dramatic context but by the uncertainty of that very context. The standard placement of the soliloquy according to the authority of the Second Quarto and the First Folio (Q2 and F1) locates the speech in III.i, after Hamlet's encounter with Rosencrantz and Guildenstern and the arrival of the players, consequently after his decision to use the Mousetrap to catch the conscience of the King. The First Quarto (Q1; the "bad" quarto) places the soliloquy in II.ii, before these events, and *Der Bestrafte Brudermord* places the interview with Ophelia, which immediately follows the soliloquy, in a manner that concurs with Q1.[3] On authority alone, the standard placement can hardly be contested, yet the "bad" reading remains alluring, if not compelling on dramaturgical grounds. "To be or not to be" is the least motivated soliloquy in the play if we look for motivation in the immediate context. We are generally satisfied that it is motivated by the whole play rather than any particular part.

The Royal Shakespeare Company, using the Q1 placement of the soliloquy in its production of *Hamlet* during the 1989 season at Stratford, has shown what a *coup de théâtre* can be achieved by aligning "To be or not to be" with Hamlet's first appearance in Act II, transformed by the antic disposition. In the Stratford production, a disheveled Mark Rylance appeared in food-stained pajamas. In this placement, the unsettledness of Hamlet's own mind is thrust to the foreground before we view the often rather composed irrationality with which he confronts others. The Q1 placement also avoids the awkward counterthrust of the speech against the momentum of the Mousetrap scheme, quickening the tempo of this rather cerebral device. Such an argument is finally likely to be more convincing to a production company than to critics protecting an intellectual investment in a figure whose mystery provides for our industry. But finally wherever the speech is placed, it evades its context. Alone among the soliloquies, it eludes the "I" to see more deeply.

We find mixed evidence in looking for philosophical progress in the speech, which in any version of the text follows the "sallied flesh" soliloquy of Act I. Hamlet has moved from an assumption that there is a divine law, God's canon, to a seemingly agnostic position, though we may regard this position as belonging to a philosophical method. His speculation about an afterlife seems curiously uninfluenced by the testimony of the ghost. If Hamlet in soliloquy ever approaches a choric function it is here, where the tragedy provokes observations on the human condition in its broadest terms. Yet paradoxically, the soliloquy is also central to our perception of Hamlet's characteristic preoccupation with consciousness. Fear of dreams in the sleep of death is the barrier to suicide: shuffling off the flesh is not a fear in itself but simply not a solution. Even the list of burdens, those of society and not Hamlet himself, focuses on offenses against the spirit: contumely, insolence, delay, despised love. The material consequences of these offenses, though evident enough, are excluded from immediate consideration.

It is difficult to disengage the most famous passage in Western literature from our traditional convictions. We have characterized as the quintessence of morbid introspection a speech that constitutes Hamlet's first attempt to generalize his experience. The soliloquy seems clearly concerned with the burdens of the common man, or the abstract human, rather than with the unique burden of the hero, the prince born to set right an ailing world. Yet this rhetorical common ground with everyman never suggests the kind of engagement that Lear finds on the heath. The sudden presence of others in Hamlet's discourse is coupled with the sudden absence of the first person singular. Even Hamlet's "we" is circumspect: the more abstract "he" is the one who might make "his quietus," might kill himself. If this is introspection, it is the introspection of writing rather than that of speech, an introspection that is already a dissociation. If writing is, in Derrida's terms, an absence of the speaking subject, this reassimilation of writing by speech suggests the ways in which language itself is finally dissociated from the speaker.[4]

The result of this dissociation of speech and speaker is inevitably a speech without immediate context regardless of where we finally decide to place it in the sequence of events. Michael Goldman has examined the problems of the speech for the actor in ways that suggest another angle of approach. For Goldman, "properly performed, the speech should give us a sense of thought as itself alive, moving within the actor's body like another character in the labyrinth of Elsinore." Goldman's contention is that Hamlet's experience creates "an ever varying pressure on his abstract speculation."[5] I would differ with this approach perhaps only by insisting on more distance between Hamlet and this abstract speculation: my formulation would be that Hamlet does not so much express his thought in these words as test a process of discourse in speaking them. The process he explores is syllogistic in spirit even if most of the premises are implicit. He poses a question and attempts to deduce the unknown from the known.

> To be, or not to be, that is the question:
> Whether 'tis nobler in the mind to suffer
> The slings and arrows of outrageous fortune,
> Or to take arms against a sea of troubles,
> And by opposing, end them.
>
> (III.i.55–59)

Hamlet's definition of the known does not allow for subjective experience. However unsuccessful the abstract process may be, it is an intellectually aggressive one, an escalation of discourse as the Mousetrap is an escalation of self-dramatization. Viewing the soliloquy thus argues a dramaturgical logic for the placement of the speech. In seeking nobility of mind in the midst of his dilemma, Hamlet seems to pursue ethics in excess, just as he seems in his advice to the players to be seeking an aesthetic excess. In both cases, Hamlet looks for perfection where adequacy would be a godsend.

In the "bad" quarto, Hamlet is reading a book before he delivers the soliloquy, a gesture that would root his speech in written discourse. Ultimately, no such material link is necessary: writing colonizes speech. Although James Calderwood has found Hamlet's soliloquies generally characterized by "interruptiveness," this soliloquy is remarkably balanced.[6] Even the "rub" is simply part of the territory, the logical result of weighing the pros and cons of death as sleep. The soliloquy begins as philosophical discourse, explores alternatives, and then comments on that discourse. The "enterprises of great pitch and motion" are not explicit in Hamlet's philosophical contemplation. Neither suicide nor regicide seems aptly described by the term. The enterprises thus described ought to be enterprises designed to change the way things are. And they are turned aside not by this particular contemplation but thus: by discourse obeying its own rules.

Hamlet's wit attacks language at the seams, at the level of the word. His soliloquies allow language to run its course, to have its say. In soliloquy, Hamlet is not so much speaking as speaking the speech. As a dramaturgical strategy, this too is an attack on language, but it is not, from the character's perspective, the kind of self-conscious attack that characterizes Hamlet's wit in dialogue. Thought, after all, ought to work, and if the social contracts signified by words like mother, father, and king have been violated, the larger contract with language ought nonetheless to be intact. But language as a series of discourses already inscribed within a social order can only exhaust itself grappling with that order. Hamlet does what he can with the interrogative mode, but ultimately his questions themselves are embedded in a tradition even when his philosophical methods are aggressive.

In Q2, "To be or not to be" is located immediately between the reports of Rosencrantz and Guildenstern to Claudius on the results of their espionage and the scene in which Ophelia serves as a spy, although perhaps a well-meaning one. The effect of the counterpoint of Hamlet's isolation to their conspiracy is enhanced by his not being immediately concerned in the speech with overthrowing Claudius. In a broader context, Hamlet is coming to terms with a world in which he must become an avenger during the same time period in which he undertakes actions that will lead to his revenge. He comes to accept in time a chain of events largely determined from the moment of the ghost's revelations. This process of acceptance is only partially dependent on the events that transpire; time itself is an important factor. The play presents us with tightly plotted action interspersed with passages of thought whose rhetoric of self-doubt we have no reason not to trust. As an audience, we are effectively drawn through the play by its pending plots and counterplots while at a different pace Hamlet sorts through his idea of what is happening.

The two paces of the play become most conspicuous in Hamlet's speeches of self-reproach. The first speech, "O what a rogue and peasant slave am I," is an astonishing effusion of self-deprecation, following as it does on the heels of what seems to be the beginning of the Mousetrap plot. The second soliloquy of this type, "How all occasions do inform against me," does indeed follow Hamlet's bungling of the opportunity for revenge, but it is troubling to an audience because it seems to posit as a model of behavior Fortinbras's expedition to battle for a parcel of ground described as not large enough to bury the casualties. Both of these speeches are best understood as concentrating the emotional undercurrent of the scenes that surround them rather than as expressing thoughts proper to the precise moment in the sequence of events when they are uttered.

Both Hamlet's emotional response to the players' recitation and his plan to use the players in a plot against the King are implicit in his reception of the players and subsequently explicit in "O what a rogue and peasant slave am I" (II.ii.550–605). Yet the soliloquy reiterates the process of conceiving the plot as though the idea were a new one. Hamlet can hardly have been surprised at the emotions evoked in him by the scene he asked the players to recite. Nor can Hamlet's special welcome to the player who will play the King and his request to insert a brief speech into the performance be construed as unrelated to the Mousetrap plot. A subtext-minded modern playwright would have preferred to afford Hamlet his opportunity to reveal his emotions immediately. The Elizabethan tendency is to proceed in more discrete units. Yet, as Marvin Rosenberg has demonstrated, the Shakespearean text may require a performed subtext.[7] Moreover those soliloquies that signal a subtext — generally the speeches of villains — caution us before the action. However, the soliloquy does not merely reiterate Hamlet's emotional subtext. Instead, it calls the attention of the audience to its own experience as the horizon of theatrical experience.

If Hamlet is to be reproached regarding his pursuit of revenge at this point in the play, it is not for doing nothing but for translating violent revenge into nonviolent inquiry. As an audience we are rewarded by his use of means that can be represented aptly in a theater. Hamlet Senior is understandably not entertained. But the theatrical experience is nonetheless affirmed as having strong powers over the human conscience. Hamlet's self-reproach then has a dual function, serving not only to reveal an emotional undercurrent of the play but to make the Mousetrap a more logical device. Ostensibly Hamlet decides on the device after invoking his intelligence ("About my brains!") because he has "heard [t]hat guilty creatures sitting at a play" are moved to remorse. More directly, we see that Hamlet is moved strongly by theatrical mimesis and thus believes in the efficacy of his plan to evoke the same response in Claudius. The power of theater is confirmed.

Because Hamlet's Mousetrap plot goes awry, the second soliloquy of self-reproach, "How all occasions do inform against me," is not improbably timed (IV.iv.32–66). It is occasioned, however, by a strained coincidence as the muted subplot of Fortinbras's war briefly crosses the main plot. This soliloquy, which appears only in the Second Quarto, is a common candidate for deletion in performance. The speech itself is fraught with paradox. Hamlet praises Fortinbras's search for honor, but only in terms that make us condemn it. The Norwegian captain disdains the ground fought for as farmland not worth five ducats to rent. The comparative worthlessness of the land is given more rhetorical weight than the honor to be obtained. There is an appeal to finding "quarrel in a straw / When honor's at the stake," but the Norwegian soldiers ultimately fight for a "fantasy and trick of fame." That Hamlet should be provoked to shame by watching an army rush to death on a slender pretext is plausible as an emotional response, but we are not led to prefer their valor to his scruples.

Hamlet's argument concerning what it is to be a man is similarly muddy. Man is distinguished from beast by his inquiring intellect.

> What is a man,
> If his chief good and market of his time
> Be but to sleep and feed? a beast, no more.
> Sure He that made us with such large discourse,
> Looking before and after, gave us not
> That capability and godlike reason
> To fust in us unus'd.
>
>   (IV.iv.33–39)

Yet, though bestial oblivion is a possible source of inaction, it is not a plausible explanation for Hamlet's hyperconsciousness, nor is it given rhetorical weight in the soliloquies. The point of distinguishing man from beast by his reason is blunted because it is evident, at least to Hamlet's audience, that his failure to act is quintessentially human. Hamlet recommends himself to us by what he upbraids in himself. The delicacy for which he reproaches himself here is far from evident in the dramatic context of the speech. Hamlet has just completed the accidental slaughter of Polonius and the violent chastisement of his mother. He leaves for England, attended, presumably guarded: the King is unlikely to afford him an opportunity to strike. The speech only makes sense when it is viewed as a reflection on all the events preceding the sea voyage. For the last time, soliloquy forcibly draws our attention to a divided Hamlet who is not fully represented by his actions. Preceding as it does Hamlet's only prolonged absence from the stage, the speech effectively summarizes a phase of experience.

Those of Hamlet's soliloquies which remain to be discussed are those immediately tied to the plot, providing us with necessary links between actions. They speak less generally for the play as a whole and figure less prominently in the critical history of the play. Hamlet's response to the ghost constitutes such a soliloquy (I.v.92–112).

> O all you host of Heaven! O earth! What else?
> And shall I couple hell? O fie, hold, hold, my heart
> And you, my sinows, grow not instant old,
> But bear me stiffly up. Remember thee!
> Ay, thou poor ghost, whiles memory holds a seat
> In this distracted globe.
>
> (I.v.92–97)

The speech is a direct reply to the ghost's last words, but spoken with the knowledge that he has gone. In the emptiness of the stage Hamlet can address his father ("poor ghost"), his mother ("most pernicious woman"), his uncle ("smiling damned villain"), and himself. Hamlet pledges himself to what is in essence a purging of his memory. Were he to follow through on such a pledge, not only would an audience be deprived of all that we find interesting in Hamlet, but within the narrative he would be deprived of the very resources necessary to overthrow the King.

> Yea, from the table of my memory
> I'll wipe away all trivial fond records,
> All saws of books, all forms, all pressures past
> That youth and observation copied there.
>
> (I.v.98–101)

For the moment the world makes sense to Hamlet: its evil is at last explicit. He has just dared to address the ghost; he cannot yet reproach himself with delay; he exhales his pent-up anger. But the moment of emotional focus is inherently unstable: Hamlet has proposed to obliterate memory by an act of memory. The setting furthers the sense of isolation that pervades all soliloquies: alone on the battlements, he is even aban-doned by his father's absence (if we may so name the ghost). His engagement is simultaneous with his disengagement: even in his refer-ence to his "tables," he disengages himself by the act of writing.[8]

The soliloquies which we have not yet discussed are both integral to the events following the Mousetrap. One expresses the intentions with which he approaches his mother; the other explains his refusal to slay Claudius at prayer. These speeches are less suggestive of disengagement than the other soliloquies. Still, to the extent that Hamlet allows discourse its say, they are hybrids. The soliloquy "Tis now the very witching time of night" begins by touching base with the atmospheric traits of revenge tragedy and indicating the characteristics of the avenger's oath (III.ii.388–99).

> 'Tis now the very witching time of night,
> When churchyards yawn and hell itself breathes out
> Contagion to this world. Now could I drink hot blood,
> And do such bitter business as the day
> Would quake to look on.
>
> (III.ii.388–91)

To the extent that the speech is an oath, however, it is an oath about the limits Hamlet will set to his actions in the closet scene with Gertrude. His behavior will not be entirely pretense: the anger he will express is genuine. But his speech will lead Gertrude to fear for her life when her life is not threatened. As with the Mousetrap play, the audience is informed of the intention behind an act of dramatization. This kind of resolution, not quite a simple decision, not quite a formal oath, is a com-mon form of conveying intention by soliloquy. Such a resolution reveals the elements of the decision — the alternatives of murder and verbal confrontation — but the rhetorical form indicates a decision already made: "I will speak daggers to her, but use none."

More problematic is the soliloquy in which Hamlet decides not to kill Claudius (III.iii.73–96). Hamlet's predictably conditional "Now might I do it" is succeeded by a present intention, "And now I'll do't." As Hamlet "scans" the plan, we may presume he does so with a drawn sword sheathed only on his decision, "Up sword." Most unusually, Hamlet is not alone, nor is he substantially separated from the other char-acter onstage. Claudius must not only be onstage but in range of

Hamlet's sword and menaced by Hamlet's decision to kill him. Because of this other presence, the privileged relationship between the audience and the protagonist in soliloquy is subverted, not only by the abnormal integration of the soliloquy into the dramatic action but by Claudius's rival perspective on events, which brackets Hamlet's speech. Moreover, Hamlet's complicated reasoning, his exhaustion of discourse, lacks credibility in so active a situation. (Classifying the speech as an extended aside has no effect on the stage reality and leaves us with the same problems of reception.) We are left with an interpretive division. A majority seem to feel the reasoning is a plausible excuse for Hamlet's praiseworthy unwillingness to murder in cold blood. A minority find Hamlet pursuing revenge in as calculating a manner as the speech would suggest. (The theatrical effectiveness of the scene rests on neither interpretation but on the irony produced by the audience's awareness that Claudius cannot repent his crimes.) Interpretation is difficult because an instant of decision is expressed in a form almost indistinguishable from the usual discursive style of Hamlet's soliloquies. The decision is made when the words "And now I'll do't" are not accompanied by a sword stroke. The rest of the speech conveys how Hamlet reconciles himself to a decision he has already made. It is easy to see in his "scanning" not a genuine process of analysis but a formal demonstration of the absurdity of the situation.

> And now I'll do't — and so 'a goes to heaven,
> And so am I reveng'd. That would be scann'd:
> A villain kills my father, and for that
> I, his sole son, do this same villain send
> To heaven.

(III.iii.74–78)

As an audience we do not require Hamlet to justify avoiding an action we would find abhorrent.[9] We merely need the decision made plausible. As interpreters we are more demanding and consequently more frustrated in dealing with the only soliloquy in the play which directly addresses the "now" of the dramatic action.

Each soliloquy demands that we determine the breadth of its focus and its relation to action. Soliloquies in *Hamlet* range from broad retrospective views of the action of the play to tightly focused explanations of immediate intentions. In several cases, the soliloquies convey the emotional undercurrents of scenes that immediately precede them. With the exception of the soliloquy just noted, the soliloquies are not properly perceived as events in the drama, that is, as acts (even verbal acts) presumed to occur at the moment of the play when they are presented. Although the soliloquies comment on the chain of events, they are not to be taken without reservation as links in that chain.

For all the variety of purposes of the soliloquies in *Hamlet*, they speak to only some of the issues within the play. In particular, both rhetorically and as performance phenomena, they are heavily biased to Hamlet's sense of isolation and victimization. His resourcefulness and resiliency are conveyed elsewhere. Most conspicuously, because soliloquies are no longer used after the sea voyage, they do not speak for Hamlet's final relationship with the world.

It is essential that we ask anew how we receive the soliloquy in the theater. No other element of the text is so transformed by the performance text. In the theater today we can find a range of acting styles for soliloquy ranging from a poetic musing to a psychological implosion. No other element of Shakespearean drama has been so affected by modernism, from the conventions of self-revelation in psychoanalysis to the conventions of the stream-of-consciousness novel. Moreover, the development of media has affected our reception of the spoken word. In the age of television, nothing is less remarkable than the broadcasting of talk, which in a radical way is what the actor does with soliloquy.

The soliloquy has a tenuous relationship to the mimetic process of the play. In general, it is difficult to determine what soliloquy imitates, operating as it does in two worlds at once. In musing over the soliloquy, we are apt to mystify it. Calderwood, for instance, asserts, "Asides and soliloquies are duplicitous creatures capable of chameleonlike reversibility between speech and silence." [10] Our theatrical experience is quite the opposite of our musings: we await the soliloquies, expecting the actors to establish themselves there if anywhere. A long tradition of performance leads us to expect an aria of emotions, and we are seldom disappointed. The text would lead us toward silence (we seem inclined that way in cinematic soliloquy), but the stage will not have it.

Erving Goffman has suggested that soliloquy is a form of self-talk, that private pleasure forbidden and disguised in public. As such, it would clandestinely appropriate an implied audience, or an implied speaker, a "monitoring voice." [11] In part, by trying out discourses, Hamlet is appropriating a monitoring voice, but it would be difficult to find the tentative quality of self-talk on the stage. Whether it delivers rhetoric or psychology, the stage delivers an inevitably robust soliloquy. The exchange of energy between a single actor and the audience is at its peak: no ensemble shares the attention of the audience. Members of the audience find themselves singled out both by the actor's shifting focus in addressing the space of the audience and in the invitation to one-to-one correspondence implied by the actor's isolation and the absence of the multiple perspectives which are generated by dialogue. John Barton states the relationship quite simply: "If the actor shares the speech it will work. If he doesn't it'll be dissipated, and the audience won't listen properly." [12]

On the stage today, the understated performance of soliloquy, more common in England than in America, retains its power to surprise. Whether or not a soliloquy is a dramatized self-debate, it always reflects a tension between the emotions which generate it and the power of language to formulate. What I have called in *Hamlet* "giving discourse its say" is always an element in soliloquy. The stage is cleared for words and yet finally we must return to something else, a further engagement. To the extent that the soliloquy aspires to the self-sufficiency of writing, it fails the speaker. If that speaker is already grappling with emotions, the unimpassioned soliloquy will angle for them. Despite the differences in styles of performance we find in the theater, we will always find, in this tension between emotion and language, a common ground.

It is remarkable that Shakespeare's greatest tragedies, *Hamlet* and *Lear,* present us with the protagonist most known for soliloquy and the protagonist without significant soliloquy. (Lear has a moment alone before following the fool to shelter.) Though both protagonists deal with the disintegration of language as a result of social disorder whose nexus is simultaneously the family and the seat of sovereignty over the state, only Hamlet, the Wittenberg scholar, has a faith in language to lose and regain. In the midst of his disillusionment, Hamlet is still moved to inscribe the King's villainy in his tablet, to read books he no longer believes in, to prepare the players to "speak the speech." Finally, of course, control over the narrative of his life, through Horatio, becomes all he has left.

The undercurrent of lost faith that touches each of the soliloquies alienates Hamlet from his own words in ways that are understated by isolating the texts of the soliloquies for examination. The contrast between the fundamentally conventional strategies of language used in the soliloquies and the strategies of wit which surround them can only emphasize the aberration inherent in each. What is dramatic about the soliloquies is finally not the delicacy of their thought but the energy with which they disengage a line of discourse from the muddled whole. Geoffrey Hartman has maintained, "The very production of speech may depend on a disentangling of blessing and curse, on the outwitting of that eternal complex."[13] Thus understood, the soliloquies are an analytic process which through persistence breaks down that "eternal complex." In Act V of *Hamlet*, communication with Horatio becomes Hamlet's most important form of speech, and he speaks more to bless than to curse. The possibility of communication, of intersubjectivity through language, is reaffirmed. Hamlet converses with Horatio throughout the play, but until Act V, these conversations are not an affirmation of the power of language. Only in Act V does it become important to Hamlet to communicate to Horatio not only his grievances and strategies but his moods and his memories, his philosophy and his story.

Early in this chapter I suggested that soliloquy, in general, allows the spectator the same privilege that perspective allows. We might add at this point that multiple soliloquy offers the same challenge as multiple perspective, in which points of view are alternately privileged. Alternative vantage points, characteristic of Northern European (especially Dutch) art, afford the spectator the pleasure of discovery without the illusion of omnipotence. [14] In our experience of Hamlet's soliloquies, our discovery is always in part a discovery of limitations.

Part III
Theatrical Expectations

5

Body, Actor, and Character in *Hamlet*

Hamlet is a play we consistently wish to see performed. Moreover, we greet performances with an expectation of success. We expect to see the play creatively renewed yet recognizably "a *Hamlet*." That so intuitively normal a relationship of text to performance should be considered remarkable is a reflection of our contemporary rethinking of such relationships. As semiology develops the means to describe the performance text — that is, the form of the performance itself — we no longer feel justified in subordinating performance to the text in our critical analyses of the play. Consequently, we feel that the analysis of the literary text is always a truncation, yet we also feel that the analysis of the performance text is always an ossification of the immediacy of performance. Yet another line of inquiry, based in linguistics, explores ways in which the language of drama is bound to the performance process, and hence to the here and now. At the risk of hyperbole, we might say the dramatic text summons a theater, which is not to say it completely controls the performance text. [1]

No single play will serve as a paradigm for the relation of dramatic text to performance text because there is no single relationship to be conveyed. Twentieth-century theatrical practice has in large measure dedicated itself to forging new relationships. The abstract struggle between logos and performance becomes in political terms the struggle between playwright and director for artistic authorship of the performance, or a similar struggle between an ensemble and its director. Dwarfing these struggles is the emergence of the actor or actress as "star," potentially relegating an entire performance to the status of foil for an extratextual

111

personality which has become a cultural icon. For all its epistemological shifts and political shiftiness, however, the theater tends to expand its range of expression rather than to replace form with form. A play like *Hamlet* continues to resonate in the repertory, affecting our evolving sense of the possibilities of theater.

In its continual concern with the body, *Hamlet* anticipates performance by privileging the actor's bodily presence as the most important focus of the dialogue. That the body speaks about itself certainly implies that the language of the play makes an intensified reference to the here and now (that is, that the language is deictic, in linguistic terms). But we must ask if this language renders the body itself redundant. That the stage uses a body to represent a body (the actor's for the character's) has seemed to theoreticians something of an embarrassment, even when the actor's practice seemed remarkable. The theatrical experience, however, has been that the actor becomes at least two in one, actor and character, both in his own perception, as Diderot's paradox observes, and in the perception of the audience, which for much of Western theatrical history has enjoyed a theater that was both mimetic and self-referential.[2] The pleasure we take in the performance of *Hamlet* is a particular intensification of the pleasure we generally take in the immediate, felt multireferentiality of the body in theatrical performance.

The body is not merely a theatrical sign placed in congruence with the drama as literary text. Rather, the body is the presupposed ground of the text and controls the structure of the text in ways that literary analysis may fail to acknowledge. The fundamentally literary discussion of dramatic character has traditionally depended on the formulation in Aristotle's *Poetics* that defines character in terms of significant choice. But the dominant bias of Aristotle's argument is to demonstrate the ethical value of tragedy, and his bias does not necessarily correspond to that of the theater. It is arguable, for example, that ethical ambiguity is more valuable to the theater than ethical determinacy. In practice, the body has provided the ground that allows us to assimilate discontinuities of behavior while viewing a play, perhaps accumulating them for subsequent analysis. We may formulate and reformulate explanations of Hamlet's character or personality without losing sight of his fundamental theatrical coherence.

Acknowledging the body as ground, I wish to investigate three aspects of how the dramatic text of *Hamlet* points toward its embodiment in the

theater. I will examine the theatrical consequences of grounding character, personality, or identity in bodily presence. I will explore the dramatic
text as a map of gestures, and hence a plan for shaping our bodily reception of the theatrical performance. Finally, I will examine our reception
of Hamlet's passage from rejecting the body to accepting lived bodiliness, an experience that explains much of our ongoing interest in a play
that engages us only marginally in its immediate ethical conflicts.

Hamlet is the most formidable role in Western theater. No other role
so obviously beckons to the actor as the ultimate test of his talents. None,
save perhaps that of Lear is so psychologically exhausting. And no role
has so tempted actresses of genius to cross the boundaries of gender. For
all Hamlet's homiletic denunciation of women, in large measure his
character is grounded in an ungendered bodily presence: Hamlet's masculinity is defined and put at issue in social rather than biological terms.[3]
Because masculinity is problematized, actresses who undertake this role
are required to perform the male role as Hamlet is required to perform it,
rather than as a purely extraneous precondition to playing Hamlet. The
actress is thus empowered on the contemporary stage, as the actor was
empowered on the Elizabethan stage, with the opportunity to represent
the "other" gender. Most of the time, of course, no such cross-gender
casting occurs. Nonetheless, the actor, deprived of such totalizing male
roles as lover, warrior, and ruler, must approach Hamlet's masculinity as
analytically as does the actress.

The tendency of the role of Hamlet to disintegrate is a part of its
allure. Because the protagonist evolves within the self-chosen role of
madness, the actor or actress is compelled to radical discontinuity, at the
very least to discontinuity between the antic illogic of Hamlet's public
speech and the more rational rhetoric of his soliloquies and his conversations with Horatio. Whether we regard Hamlet's madness as merely put
on, or put on to disguise its coming on, it remains a theatrical madness,
incorporating conventional signs whereby his (onstage or offstage) audience perceives him as mad. The moments which contrast with this
performed madness emerge as opportunities for establishing theatrical
norms of natural behavior. An inevitable play of performance styles is
established.

If, as Jean Alter suggests, survival of a dramatic text in the theater
depends in part on its variability in performance, then the characteristic
"play" within the role of Hamlet contributes strongly to the inexhaustible

vitality of the text. Alter defines a play with "a high index of theatrality" as one which may be transformed by performance "to project ever new referents."[4] At the same time, he maintains, the coherence of a play depends on the integration of its referential elements — that is, on their mutual interdependence for meaning. The vitality of *Hamlet* is not at issue. The coherence of the play has been questioned, however, for the most part by those who wish to anchor the play to a set of fixed referents — that is, to define (and implicitly to control) its meaning. In Alter's terms, coherence demands not that the referents remain the same but that they remain integrated. Because Hamlet is defined in the theater through an alternation between moments of sane and insane behavior, a degree of coherence is provided by the pattern in which these behaviors are perceived (always in relation to each other). Inevitably, the performance of both madness and normalcy will vary according to evolving cultural codes and theatrical codes. But the ratio of performance styles gives the play stability of form without an ossification of meaning.

In the theater, we initially assume a unity of person for a dramatic character. That is, we agree to assume that we see a person before we can begin to define or even describe that person's behavior: The character is there before being constituted by the text. If centuries of source study have demonstrated anything, it is that the Shakespearean text is a cross-roads of appropriated narratives and discourses without a common axiomatic ground. The unity of person becomes a ground for the project of constructing personality, a project only partially accomplished by the dramatic text. The verbal promiscuity of the character Hamlet is the net result of grouping together heterogeneous utterances less remarkable in themselves than in their juxtaposition. We agree to consider that juxta-position intriguing rather than incompetent. The process whereby we unify the dramatic character is not completely different from that whereby we unify narrative characters, but it is different in degree and more fundamentally tolerant of discontinuity because it is anchored in the biological continuity of the actor rather than in the linear continuity of the text. Moreover, we are accustomed to reconciling our reading of a given play to our experience of playgoing; that is, we read a play with an analogous permissiveness. It is more difficult, however, to reconcile such permissiveness with analytic procedures.

Recent efforts at rehabilitating the concept of representation suggest some of the difficulties of isolating the literary text. Two recent studies of mimesis examine ways in which the Shakespearean text constitutes an extension or interrogation of received conventions. Howard Felperin's *Shakespearean Representation* views Shakespeare as a "mediator of theatrical change" in his juxtaposition of archaic and more naturalistic theatrical modes.[5] But his close examination of the text foregrounds the contrast of these modes at the expense of the integrating capacity of performance. In *A New Mimesis*, A. D. Nuttall examines the relation to reality of Shakespearean texts as "fictitious literature."[6] His philosophical justification of an informed "transparent criticism," which looks through formal structures rather than at them, consistently compares verbal structure with pictorial art, circumventing the stage embodiment. His purely literary reading conflates the visible production with the field of pure verbal representation: mimesis and diegesis are not distinguished.

The theoretical stance that isolates the dramatic text as literary text has serious interpretive consequences. The diversity of dramatic modes in *Hamlet* is far less disruptive for an audience than is the diversity of narrative modes in James Joyce's *Ulysses*. But though Felperin argues convincingly that Shakespeare opens "inherited dramatic models to invite, even demand, other models of understanding, including those we use on people we know,"[7] his foregrounding of the medieval legacy becomes a kind of novelization of the play. Felperin suggests of the closet scene:

> The only trouble is that the closet scene is in certain respects not less archaic and anti-mimetic than the play scene, but more so. Despite its attractiveness to nineteenth-century characterological and twentieth-century psychoanalytic critics, the closet scene tells us little about Hamlet's alleged state of mind. For most of the scene he does not speak as a son to his mother at all, but as a preacher to a sinner, not out of personal feeling but out of impersonal *indignatio*. (49)

But like the dog who did nothing in the night, that is the curious incident. Within the play, Hamlet's homiletic style is consistently viewed by other characters in the play as unnatural behavior. Gertrude's conscience is awakened by the sermon, but so is her fear for the sanity of the sermonizing Prince. The events of the closet scene are complicated by a ghostly visitation and a killing, but Hamlet's earlier confrontation with Ophelia provokes a similar reaction to his inappropriate sermonizing.

> *Hamlet.* I have heard of your paintings well enough. God hath
> given you one face, and you make yourselves another. You
> jig and amble, and you lisp, you nickname God's creatures
> and make your wantonness your ignorance. Go to, I'll no
> more on't, it hath made me mad. I say we will have no moe
> marriage. Those that are married already (all but one) shall
> live, the rest shall keep as they are. To a nunn'ry, go.
> *Ophelia.* O, what a noble mind is here o'erthrown!
> The courtier's, soldier's, scholar's, eye, tongue, sword,
> Th'expcctation and rose of the fair state,
> The glass of fashion and the mould of form,
> Th'observed of all observers, quite, quite, down!
>
> (III.i.142–54)

The appropriation of the homiletic text by the Prince is judged mad, as
is Ophelia's appropriation of the text of a bawdy ballad later in the play.
At the metadramatic level, the reader or audience is indeed aware of the
play of texts. But the play of texts is possible because the project of
maintaining the coherence of the fiction is so permissive. Through the
body of the actor or, in reading, the presumed bodily source of every
utterance, the character is already there.

Though the actor's bodily presence serves as the ground of our
perception, this ground itself is subject to an evolving conceptualization.
Wladimir Krysinski has explored the impact of this evolving conceptualization on the modalities of the body.

> The problem of the body in modern theater is, within acceptable proportion,
> parallel to the evolution of the body in modern thought and philosophy. To
> the same extent that philosophical reflection on the body rids itself of the
> Cartesian dualities to posit the body, ultimately, as an object in itself as
> Leiblichkeit, [lived bodiliness], so modern theater also effects a considerable
> displacement of the body. The body, formerly the somatic support for a
> discursive logos, becomes the sign proper, the support for a theatricality
> which transcends psychological theater.[8]

How can *Hamlet* be placed in the context of this argument? Krysinski
locates in the modern theater a rupture between the textual or scenic
corpus, defined in terms of representational codes, and the body itself,
charged with instinctual energy. As philosophy reintegrated mind and
body, or at least problematized their relationship, the theater became less

willing to allow the body to be assimilated by discourse. Chronologi-
cally, *Hamlet* precedes Cartesian dualism and thus avoids at least the
institutionalized objectification of the body.[9] Moreover, Renaissance
conceptions of the relation of body to soul are sufficiently problematic to
preclude a systematically dualistic theological perspective: somewhere at
the margins of Neoplatonism lies the risk of Manichaeism. The public
stage would have been a particularly unlikely and perilous forum for
systematically unorthodox theology. Such an argument is circumstantial;
more significant is the theatrical practice wherein the actor's body is
consistently multireferential. The metatheatrical dimension of Elizabethan and Jacobean theater, which has received sustained critical attention since Lionel Abel's *Metatheatre* (1963), serves to draw attention to
mimetic activity as "real" activity, and consequently to multiply readings
of the actor's body.[10] The simplest understanding of the effect of
metatheatrical references would be that we might consider the actor as
character *or* as actor. But the readings may be simultaneous as well as
alternative, and furthermore the staged actor, the actor performing his
self-reference, may also be seen as a kind of fiction. Moreover, a symbolic reading of the actor may at a given moment be made to emerge by
an evocation of the allegorical tradition.

In *Hamlet*, a discourse about the body emanates from the body, and
the principal point of that discourse is that it has not solved the body. The
soliloquies periodically view death as the only possible exit from insolu-
ble philosophical problems, but they do not anticipate that vantage point.
(Significantly, when Hamlet dies, the discourse is silence.) It is impossible to isolate the body as object of the discourse or to assume a discourse
that would define the body textually. A difference between words about
the body and the body itself is essential to the dramaturgy of *Hamlet*.

The actor's presence is in itself a source of continuity for an audience.
His body may well be used at times as "the somatic support for a discursive logos," in Krysinski's terms, but it may also be sufficient to sustain a
pre-discursive chaos. The continuous being of the actor may validate the
identity of a character whose conformity to a psychological model is not
established by the words and gestures which constitute "the part." The
character is "played" rather than "communicated." The logical discontinuities allowed in the dramatic text may be of value in themselves as a
means of displaying conflicts between (and within) the models of
personality posited by philosophy and psychology.

The actor's presence organizes theatrical discourse around the zero point "I/here."[11] In using the term "presence" as a measure of the actor's artistry, we proclaim the centrality to the theatrical experience of the actor's ability to project himself, to manifest this I/here everywhere in the theater; in Joseph Chaikin's words, presence is "a quality that makes you feel as though you're standing right next to the actor."[12] The actor's "I" is both I-as-character, present through mimesis, and I-as-actor, present in the act of mimesis. The actor's "here" is both the mimetic space — the scene — and the theater, which, as framework, provides space for mimesis. In part, the alternation between mimesis and self-reference is denoted by the dramatic text: metadramatic references in the text clearly suggest actor/theater, and, in the main, a realistic text suggests character/scene. But at any moment an actor's virtuosity in mimesis may manifest rather than conceal his presence as actor. Although the text can never entirely orchestrate the reception of this doubleness of person and place in the theater, the text may assume this doubleness as context.

The doubly perceived I/here of the actor is sustained by the gestures, including verbal gestures, by which the actor focuses attention on himself. A dramatic text continually provides for this focus on the actor's bodily presence. (This is not to say that the text provides every detail, or every gesture, of performance.) Traditionally, the most common reason to focus on an actor has been because he is saying something. Consequently, the study of dramatic texts has noted the predominance of speech acts — speech through which the speaker accomplishes an action, foregrounding the "I" — and of deixis, speech which points to the immediate scene, anchoring the actor in the "here."[13] Though there are radical distinctions between reading a text and attending a performance, I would suggest that if speech dominates a play, we can have an experience called "reading the play." If not, and twentieth-century theater provides a host of such plays, we can at best read the script, as we can read a filmscript without feeling that we have read a film by so doing. The distinction does not depend on how precisely the text defines the performance. For example, in his late plays Beckett may completely define a stage representation, but because the signs he defines are nonverbal, any experience of the play awaits performance.

Although the act of reading the word-dominated play is significantly related to performance, performance is not simply a change of medium. Questioning the classical concept of "translating" the text to theatrical terms, Anne Ubersfeld observes that such an idea depends on the assumption that the materiality of the signifier has no effect on meaning.[14] Nor is the actor merely conveying the play's words as message. Patrice Pavis argues that the application of communication theories to the relation of stage to audience is futile because signs originating within a closed fiction are not simply "exchanged" with spectators perceiving the fictional event.[15] At the very least, it is difficult to partition the communication of the fiction from the spectators' response. Elam observes, "the actor-spectator transaction within the *theatrical* context is mediated by a *dramatic* context in which a fictional speaker addresses a fictional listener"[16] As an oblique but provocative illustration of the distinction between performance and message, consider the role of the messenger on the stage. We think immediately of a mumbling extra whose every moment onstage is an agony for himself and his audience because he cannot justify his physical presence. His "I" is dominated by the message of another, and his body loiters until directed offstage. *Hamlet*'s conspicuous messenger, Osric, is so playable a character because he is so bad a messenger, obscuring information with the noise of his own prattle.

Stage presence — I/here — requires continual renewal; that is, presence is performed, not denoted. This necessity derives from the conditions of theater: theater practice has established that the onstage body must be justified. As Bert States observes, the body cannot be imaginatively "put on hold" like other objects on the stage.[17] The necessity of justifying the actor's body leads to, or corresponds to, a continual justification of the character's presence. The same gestures sustain the dual presence of actor/character. While it is possible that a stage character's gestures are entirely motivated by the plot, there is a tendency for the actor/character to be drawn into a conspicuous performance of his presence, which becomes as well what Joseph Chaikin calls a performance of person, a recommendation of "a way of making oneself visible, recognizable, and comprehensible to another."[18] In *Hamlet,* the process of performing presence and person is fundamentally paradoxical. At one time or another the protagonist desires to be invisible, unrecognizable, and incomprehensible.

We may justifiably be suspicious of the transition between the formal concept, performance of presence, and the more obviously ideological one, performance of person. Such a transition is justified to the extent that the society described conceives of its behavior in theatrical terms and views its theater as mimetic. If this situation obtains, then a character performing his presence is behaving in a way compatible with realism: his way of behaving is part of the plot. When "All the world's a stage" seems a cogent observation, we are justified in discussing the performance of person.

What is most conspicuous about Hamlet as a character is that he performs his presence while desiring and in part by desiring his absence. And that presence is pervasive. During the period before his absence from Elsinore, every scene in which Hamlet does not appear either points toward his entrance or makes him present narratively. In I.i, the ghost appears and Hamlet must be informed; in I.iii, Ophelia is warned against Hamlet's affections by her brother and father. In II.i, Ophelia narrates Hamlet's dumb show; in IV.i, Gertrude narrates Hamlet's killing of Polonius. During Hamlet's absence from Elsinore, IV.v-vii, the last two scenes revolve around letters announcing his imminent arrival. Only in IV.v (the scene of Ophelia's madness and Laertes' return) is Hamlet absent and unnamed, but there his causal relationship to the events makes the omission seem a repression.

It is ideologically significant that the dramatic text concerns itself with presence. Harry Berger argues that there is a provocative tension between Shakespearean text and performance through which "we alternately reproduce and question the community's imaginative achievement." [19] Examining the ideologies of text and performance, Berger asserts that because the referent of a character's name is unassigned in the text, this absence of an embodied representation "opens the character's unmediated absence to our representation" and ultimately permits dislocation that challenges "the individualism of speakers" (53-54). But although textuality is implicit in Shakespeare's language, as Berger asserts, so is a dialogical relationship of presence and absence that distinguishes between language through which presence is performed and language which specifies absence. Where the dialogue of presence and absence is central — in *Hamlet*, in *Antony and Cleopatra*, in *Lear*, or in *Twelfth Night* — we cannot read the text as undifferentiated absence without diffusing the central dramatic tensions.

The process through which Hamlet performs his presence, and his person, undergoes an evolution which can be traced through the array of theatrical activities which seem so disconnected from the kind of violent action which he must undertake. These theatrical activities may be seen to activate and ultimately to transform him. In Chaikin's terms, he recommends a mode of behavior to himself. Maurice Merleau-Ponty's formulations of how the body functions in expression and speech strongly suggest the ways in which theater affects Hamlet as well as the ways in which it is his instrument. [20] Merleau-Ponty's description of how gesture is perceived suggests how presence works on the observer.

> The communication or comprehension of gestures comes about through the reciprocity of my intentions and the gestures of others, of my gestures and intentions discernible in the conduct of other people. It is as if the other person's intention inhabited my body and mine his. The gesture which I witness outlines an intentional object. This object is genuinely present and fully comprehended when the powers of my body adjust themselves to it and overlap it. The gesture presents itself to me as a question, bringing certain perceptible bits of the world to my notice, and inviting my concurrence in them. Communication is achieved when my conduct identifies this path with its own. (185)

The question posed by the actor's gesture wreaks such emotional havoc in Hamlet, and subsequently in Claudius, because each is so disposed to bodily reciprocity with the events enacted. Hamlet's grief and Claudius's guilt are summoned to inhabit their bodies. Hamlet seems fitfully aware that acting produces such an effect. Certainly his Mouse-trap play is predicated on the predictability of the King's guilty response. Hamlet seems almost equally to anticipate the Queen's response, but he is less explicitly aware of his own. His expectations depend more on a theory of conscience than on a theory of performance. In part, he expects to surprise the King and Queen with what he knows. But knowing the text of the play, Hamlet himself is nonetheless moved by the performance and not just by the King's consternation. Merleau-Ponty's formulation of how we comprehend gestures explains how an actor can project his presence in the theater: for the audience he is not outside, but within. For those who watch the Mousetrap at Elsinore, however, little virtuosity is required of the players. The performance is, like the Last Judgement, already within.

Hamlet himself poses two seemingly incompatible theories of acting. [21] His oft-cited advice to the players advocates moderation and decorum. His decision to stage the Mousetrap, however, is couched in a soliloquy that seems to propose an almost Artaudian model of the theater

— a theater that transports and transforms its audience like the plague.[22] Hamlet marvels at the player who "but in a fiction, in a dream of passion, / Could force his soul so to his own conceit ... his whole function suiting / With forms to his conceit." Had the player Hamlet's "motive," he would "cleave the general ear with horrid speech, / Make mad the guilty, and appall the free." Properly motivated, the player would, in effect, perpetrate an earsplitting violation of Hamlet's own subsequent advice to the players. But this earsplitting actor is only a preliminary conception, almost a metaphorical one. Finally, it is not in the players' performance but in the reception of the play that the guilty are made mad, and that reception depends on the play's language, on its specification of violated oaths. A certain moderation is essential to speech; the potency of language is not proportional to its volume. What Hamlet remembers of the players' previous visit is not mere passion but a passionate speech, and he resorts to "a speech of some dozen lines, or sixteen lines" to sharpen the resemblance of "The Murder of Gonzago" to his father's murder. Hamlet's theories about the theater are reconciled in his design of the Mousetrap. His theories will not, however, allow him to control his own response to the performance he has (in effect) directed.

In ascribing power to speech, we are not disavowing our sense of the actor's presence but extending it. In Merleau-Ponty's understanding of gesture, which we have applied to theater, speech is also perceived as gesture, as a relation of body to body.

> The spoken word is a genuine gesture, and it contains its meaning in the same way as the gesture contains its. This is what makes communication possible. In order that I may understand the words of another person, it is clear that his vocabulary and syntax must be "already known" to me. But that does not mean that words do their work by arousing in me "representations" associated with them, and which in aggregate eventually reproduce in me the original "representation" of the speaker. What I communicate with primarily is not "representations" or thought, but a speaking subject, with a certain style of being and with the "world" at which he directs his aim.[23]

In a play in which speech is the dominant gesture, the dialogue maps most of the relationship of auditor's body to actor's — that is, the identification of intention with a speaking subject. The identification of the body in the theater is not a constant to be considered by the text, but a variable strongly responsive to the text's own variations. Communication, as construed by Merleau-Ponty, is constituted by a relationship rather than an exchange of messages. The audience's relationship to the speaking subject does not depend on its being addressed by the speaker, as in general it is not, but on its aligning itself with the speaker's intentions and "style of being." Communication thus construed is not disrupted by the character's occupying the plane of fiction while the audience occupies the plane of the theatrical event.

Our theatrical experience of Hamlet is to trace his bodily gestures bodily. What we experience is a passage, mapped by gestures, from his intense discomfort at being in the world to his acceptance of being in the world. Because gesture is directed toward the world, Hamlet's gestures of denying the world are self-frustrating: he typically repudiates them even as he performs them. At the same time, without the reciprocity of others, all his gestures are negated: he is deprived of the mutual resonance that constitutes human life. This absence of reciprocity is at the core of what Hamlet finds unnatural. Hamlet is initially incensed at his mother's unnatural response to his father's death. But the natural emotions that he expects of himself are themselves inextricable from the cultural context — from the structure of the family, from the structure of the state — and that cultural context, that network of reciprocities, is disrupted by the incestuous royal marriage. Thus Hamlet is frustrated in his search for natural behavior. His alternative models for behavior become the animal and the artificial. His mother's behavior seems inferior to that of a beast. His own passionate response seems inferior to the player's capacity for passionate gesture, ultimately "shaped to his own conceit." Only by undertaking what he believes to be an entirely artificial behavior, a role, does he regain access to natural human behavior, that is, to his own cultural norms. Merleau-Ponty's formulation of the interaction of nature and culture aptly defines Hamlet's dilemma.

Feelings and passional conduct are invented like words. Even those which, like paternity, seem to be part and parcel of the human make-up are in reality institutions. It is impossible to superimpose on man a lower level of behavior which one chooses to call "natural," followed by a manufactured cultural or spiritual world. Everything is both manufactured and natural in man, as it were, in the sense that there is not a word, not a form of behavior which does not owe something to purely biological being — and which at the same time does not elude the simplicity of animal life, and cause forms of vital behavior to deviate from their pre-ordained direction, through a sort of *leakage* and through a genius for ambiguity which might serve to define man. (189)

To put on an antic disposition is to accept an array of forms of behavior no less cultural for being abnormal. Hamlet's riddling wit is no more or less a cultural expression of hostility than is a duel, or the hurling of a rock in the streets; but because it is both extensive and varied, the antic disposition provides for a more protracted commerce with the "natural." Hamlet's conspicuously "manufactured" behavior allows him a passional conduct until he is able to reappropriate the conventions of passional conduct from which he has been alienated.

We can see in Hamlet's two great soliloquies on death that life is reasserted by the very gestures which would deny it. The first of these soliloquies seems initially to be a kind of systematic disablement of the body and its functions. Were this speech the paradigm of Hamlet's performed presence in the play, there would be little disparity between his perception that he is inactive and our perception as audience that he is the dynamic center of the play. But Hamlet's desire that the "too too sallied flesh would melt, / Thaw, and resolve itself into a dew!" focuses attention directly on the body's presence, a presence more intense because Hamlet grapples with it. The soliloquy becomes a reiteration of the gesture he cannot help but make: "Must I remember? ... Let me not think on't!" Hamlet's conclusion suggests a complete withdrawal from the world: "It is not nor it cannot come to good, / But break my heart, for I must hold my tongue." But if we are certain of anything about Hamlet it is that he does not hold his tongue.

The soliloquy "To be or not to be" provides an even more conspicuous assertion of presence. If in the end "the native hue of resolution / Is sicklied o'er with the pale cast of thought," the speech nonetheless embodies that resolution, protests injustice. Even shuffling off the mortal coil suggests an act necessary to escape the body, a grappling with presence. Granted that the inquiry is hypothetical, hypothesizing is itself a gesture engaging the world. Hamlet's self-negating protests against "being" necessarily constitute only a limited manifestation of his desire for nonbeing. By role-playing, he is able to substitute limited scenarios for the fullness of being. The antic disposition, intended as a strategy of misdirection, serves to misdirect not only Claudius but Hamlet himself, who escapes his sense of his own presence by being another. In addition, this role-playing suggests a kind of power: Hamlet's ability to stage his antic behavior implies that the body is a governed instrument of mind or self. However, the nature of the process of performing the self calls into question so simple a separation of body from self. The protagonist's performance of self, which is manifested through the actor's performance of presence, undergoes three broad movements which bring Hamlet from inwardness (tending to self-contradiction on the stage) to self-conscious performance, and beyond that performance to an acceptance of bodily presence (performance of self without self-consciousness).

To seem is to be legible according to some rational yet arbitrary code that guides perception. Nowhere are intense feelings more bound to institutionalized behavior than in mourning. When the court at Elsinore curtails its public rituals of mourning, Hamlet is left conscious of his own coded behavior, now devoid of social context. His denunciation of seeming, an inventory of costumes and a description of stage gestures, expresses his disillusionment with the culture that provides these codes, but inevitably renounces his own behavior as well.

> Seems, Madam? nay, it is, I know not "seems."
> 'Tis not alone my inky cloak, good mother,
> Nor customary suits of solemn black,
> Nor windy suspiration of forc'd breath,
> No, nor the fruitful river in the eye,
> Nor the dejected havior of the visage,
> Together with all forms, moods, shapes of grief,
> That can denote me truly. These indeed seem,
> For they are actions that a man might play,
> But I have that within which passes show,
> These but the trappings and the suits of woe.
>
> (I.ii.76–86)

But, having defined himself in terms of an inner truth, Hamlet concludes the first act with a decision to play the antic.

Hamlet's entrance in the antic disposition is anticipated by Ophelia's description of his dumb show, a description in which we see him as master of the very gestures he has renounced.

My lord, as I was sewing in my closet,
Lord Hamlet, with his doublet all unbrac'd,
No hat upon his head, his stockings fouled,
Ungart'red, and down-gyved to his ankle,
Pale as his shirt, his knees knocking each other,
And with a look so piteous in purport
As if he had been loosed out of hell
To speak of horrors — he comes before me.

(II.i.74–81)

We are being given the key to a new stage code. The speech serves as a narrative bridge between a phase of the play in which we are being enjoined to trust Hamlet's appearance and one in which we are directed to distrust it. Yet a kind of "leakage" has begun between his manufactured and his natural emotions. How much closer to hell's horrors could he have been? How far from his "genuine" emotions are those he performs for Ophelia?[24]

The antic disposition constitutes a permission to perform irreconcilable opposites, such as the denunciation of the flesh in Hamlet's "Get thee to a nunn'ry," and the expression of desire in his banter with Ophelia at the Mousetrap play. Whereas contrary impulses play to a standstill in Hamlet's soliloquies, his public behavior expresses contrary impulses sequentially, without regard to inconsistency. These public scenarios consistently evoke the double presence of actor/character, empowering the stage figure before the play's logos has defined his power.

The relationship between playing an action and taking action is complex; at least, it is so when world and theater are not partitioned. In *Hamlet*, the value of passion as a motive to action is particularly problematic. Hamlet initially marvels at the player's "dream of passion" and imagines the effect of a player with Hamlet's own motivation (to impose a modern term). But this formulation of performance suits neither his own theory of action nor his theory of acting. His theory of action would seem to be revealed in his praise of Horatio, the man "that is not passion's slave." His address to the players similarly counsels moderation, a temperance "in the very torrent, tempest, and ... whirlwind of ... passion." Hamlet's further instructions, "Suit the action to the word, the word to the action," suggest a manufactured imitation of nature. However, the history of acting suggests the pervasiveness of what Merleau-Ponty calls "leakage" between the manufactured and the natural. Stanislavski's methodical use of emotional memory was not so much a revolution in acting as a conspicuous phase of its evolution. The body as instrument remains the body in itself.

Were the consideration of acting limited to the preparation and performance of the Mousetrap play, framed as theater within the diegesis, the preponderance of evidence in *Hamlet* would point to a theory of performance dominated by control. In accord with such a theory, the "dream of passion" would be a metaphorical description of how the actor engages emotional mechanisms rather than of how he responds emotionally. But when Hamlet follows the Mousetrap play with his own "unframed" performance in his mother's closet, his emotional state results in the death of Polonius (and as a consequence those of Ophelia and Laertes).

Hamlet's soliloquy, "'Tis now the very witching time of night," serves to inform us of his intentions in the closet scene to follow, but the contradiction between these intentions and their fatal consequences necessitates a closer look at his impassioned rhetoric.

> O heart, lose not thy nature! let not ever
> The soul of Nero enter this firm bosom,
> Let me be cruel, not unnatural;
> I will speak daggers to her, but use none.
> My tongue and soul in this be hypocrites —
> How in my words somever she be shent,
> To give them seals never my soul consent!
>
> (III.ii.393–99)

Hamlet twice invokes nature to prevent himself from committing acts of violence against his mother, yet nothing could be more unnatural for a man than for his tongue and soul to be hypocrites. The moral and emotional jeopardy in which Hamlet has placed himself is suggested by Claudius's prayer scene, which stands between the Mousetrap and the closet scene. Claudius concludes his unsuccessful attempt at prayer: "My words fly up, my thoughts remain below: / Words without thoughts never to heaven go" (III.iii.97–98). Claudius performs unsuccessfully before heaven, where "action lies / In his true nature," but he unwittingly performs successfully before Hamlet, who is misled by the King's hypocrisy for the only time in the play. The scene suggests that the consequences of action that disguises its true nature are unlikely to be as predictable as Hamlet expects. Moreover, the casebook study of hypocrisy in the King can only darken our perception of Hamlet's own studied "hypocrisy."

The inherent instability of any unframed scenario is manifested in the closet scene.[25] So quick to find reasons for inaction in the prayer scene, Hamlet seems as ready to use daggers as to speak them in his mother's closet. Hamlet's soliloquy asserts that the confrontation is a controlled performance, but his acting consists merely of giving vent to his anger against his mother. He exercises control not by constructing a pattern of word and action but by modulating the level of his passion. Yet this performance raises Hamlet to a level of excitement which results in an immediate and deadly response to Polonius's cry from behind the arras. The gap between thought and action that has incapacitated Hamlet to this point is bridged by his "acting out": the habit of acting becomes the habit of action. However, this seemingly salutary result is marred by the violation of the frame for Hamlet's acting. He casts Claudius and Gertrude in his mental scenario, but the world, in the person of Polonius, rashly intrudes.

Though Hamlet comes short of understanding his own psychological processes, the principle whereby he becomes capable of action is that which he urges Gertrude to adopt in shunning Claudius's bed: "For use almost can change the stamp of nature." Hamlet's art is "use" because his medium is his body, becoming through gesture more disposed to action. By "action" Hamlet usually intends significant physical action, ultimately "Th'important acting of [the ghost's] dread command." The term "action," however, may also refer more simply to gesture, the "piteous action" of the ghost's glare, for example. Surprisingly, given the contemplative nature of the protagonist, the philosophical range of the concept "action" is curtailed rather than expanded in the course of the play. Hamlet moves toward a disposition to action, but the play's early concerns with the purpose and efficacy of action are displaced as the protagonist surrenders the burden of his preoccupation with controlling the world.[26]

Act V marks Hamlet's reincorporation of his own behavior; he performs only himself. At Ophelia's grave site he reproaches Laertes for the gesture of leaping in her grave. Though he claims to be a match for anyone in hyperbolic gesture — he will "drink up eisel, eat a crocodile" — he comes almost full circle in denouncing such shows. Moreover, in

Act V he is willing to trust his emotions again. As Hamlet narrates to Horatio the circumstances of his dispatching Rosencrantz and Guilden-stern, he was drawn from his cabin because "in [his] heart there was a kind of fighting / That would not let [him] sleep." "Our indiscretion," he observes, "sometime serves us well / When our deep plots do pall." At the behest of his fears, he acts against his betrayers, replacing his death warrant with their own. Fear seems to rehabilitate him: on the next day he boards the pirate ship in combat. Conspicuously, when Hamlet is most capable of action, he is most susceptible to fear. His dysfunctional bravado has vanished.

In Hamlet's view, the events at sea suggest that "there's a divinity that shapes our ends, / Rough-hew them how we will." Under the aegis of what he takes to be a divine sanction of intuitive action, he is restored to a full range of emotions: passionate response to Laertes' grief, and sympathy for Laertes on reflection; misgivings at the fencing match, and anger at Claudius's final treachery. Hamlet ceases to concern himself with the codes through which his emotion is expressed. Being human, he is of a culture, but he does not feel himself to be representing his emotions according to cultural norms. Rather, he feels his emotions themselves.

At the same time, Hamlet's foil, Laertes, is in the process of encoding his emotions: stylizing his grief at his sister's funeral; forgiving Hamlet, or pretending to in nature, but preserving the right to consult the forms of honor; finally even committing a murder concealed behind the outward form of a code of arms. The point is not that Laertes is radically different from Hamlet, but rather that their potential kinship is out of phase. Laertes is assuming a role that Hamlet is in the process of vacating. Indeed, Hamlet's anger at Laertes may reflect as much self-recognition as does his subsequent sympathy. Laertes' almost parodic condensation of Hamlet's passage serves as foil not so much for Hamlet's contempla-tive character — Hamlet is not, after all, remarkably contemplative in Act V — but for his emergence into the ordinary.

What we demand to experience in seeking the performance of *Hamlet* is not the play's climactic violence or even its particular conflict of ethi-cal values. Rather, we wish to experience, through the correspondence of our bodily response to the play's bodily gestures, first a heightened consciousness of codes of behavior, and then a liberating playacting that returns us to our own lived bodiliness. The phenomenological argument of the play preserves its identity even as our perception of its cultural assumptions varies with our own.

6
Issues of Culture and Genre

Polonius introduces the players in a manner which suggests that generic classification is already, for Shakespeare's audience, a public joke.

> The best actors in the world, either for trag-
> edy, comedy, history, pastoral, pastoral-comical,
> historical-pastoral, tragical-historical, tragical-comi-
> cal-historical-pastoral, scene individable, or poem
> unlimited; Seneca cannot be too heavy, nor Plautus
> too light, for the law of writ and the liberty: these
> are the only men.
>
> (II.ii.396–402)

But even though this proliferation of genres is a public joke, the speech still constitutes a public advertisement of the kind of versatility possessed by the Elizabethan repertory company.

The devourer of narratives that was the Elizabethan theater was capable of responding to the demands of its audience with a rapidity that modern entertainment media would find difficult to duplicate. For modern production systems with similar responsiveness and flexibility, we might look to the Hollywood studio system with its integrated production and distribution facilities, or to the live productions of early television with their conventional level of rough representation. In the task of cataloguing plays, as in the Folio, Shakespeare's contemporaries remained committed to a few classical terms. Theorizing, they tended toward the kind of generic combinatorics that Polonius takes to the extreme. In a project like tragicomedy, such a theoretical combination proved theatrically fruitful.[1] However, a theater highly responsive to audience reactions also generated types of plays which our criticism and marketplace might call genres (as we call the Western a genre film) but which received no sustained critical attention at the time. Nonetheless, such types established or appropriated conventions and developed an audience competence which shaped their reception. A certain generic competence developed before ideological consistency was established. Whereas Attic tragedy reworked myths securely embedded within a culture, Elizabethan drama absorbed subject matter that varied greatly in its degree of previous ideological assimilation. The theater had obviously a greater freedom in dealing with Hamlet, Prince of Denmark, than with King Richard III of England.

The Catalogue (or table of contents) of the First Folio groups its contents under the simple categories of comedy, history, and tragedy. Almost as if to advertise its generic marginality, *Troilus and Cressida* is absent from the list (though printed with the tragedies). At the center, the histories constitute an orderly array. *King John* and *Henry VIII* frame the two tetralogies. There is historical chronology in the whole, and each tetralogy is a coherent unit of narrative. From our perspective, the rest of the catalogue is more arbitrary. The list of comedies follows no logic of subgenre or development, but the plays are what we would broadly call comedies. The list of tragedies is more chaotic. Roman history isn't history, but, being no laughing matter, is tragedy; distant British history is tragedy, even in the case of *Cymbeline*. That the division of the catalogue is arbitrary is not to say it is irrational, but the rationale of the catalogue is that of a very ideological way of determining genre. History is that which concerns Christian Englishmen. (This is not to suggest that Shakespeare took no risks in this genre.) Tragedy, all indexed with proper names, is the domain of significant masculine decision. The women who appear in titles not only settle for second billing but constitute a fatal attraction as well. *Cymbeline*, the odd entry, does conclude with the celebration of Cymbeline's peace, an act of state.[2] In the comedies, entitled with either generic or thematic names, feminine decision tends to dominate, share, or at least intervene in the decision process leading to the restoration of social order. This general trend does not in itself, of course, prevent a tragedy from challenging patriarchal order or a comedy from acceding to it.[3]

While English history had already established an ideological frame-work both in historical record and popular tradition — the Tudor myth — the miscellaneous sources of the other plays arrived with a much more disparate set of assumptions, and there were no clear proscriptions requiring their immediate assimilation to a rationalized ideology. Eventually a repeated scenario will tend to such an assimilation; such a trend is addressed by Bowers's argument that the tragedy of revenge, confined by increasingly clear moral proscriptions against revenge, degenerates toward a drama of pure villainy. (Bowers himself asserts a direct causality.)[4]

Revenge tragedy as a genre, subgenre, or generic impulse, implied certain emotional expectations which Shakespeare satisfied with *Hamlet*, others which he disappointed, but his solution as a whole was against the grain of the genre's movement toward ideological consistency and simplification of emotional response. The emotional appeal of revenge tragedy in the public theater is attributable, at least in part, to the encounter with the violent and macabre authorized by the destruction of the avenger, usually preceded by his psychological deterioration. The audience can enjoy the appeal of revenge — Bacon's "Wilde Justice" — without seeming to have made an investment in lawlessness.[5] Various academic approaches generate their own boundaries for the genre. F. L. Lucas, tracing the Senecan influence, includes such plays as *Richard III*. Prosser traces the ethical issues through academic drama. Bowers looks to Kyd's *The Spanish Tragedy* as a *locus classicus* of the generic charac-teristics.[6] My concern is not to establish a canon of plays but to consider the broad expectations of the public theater audience that are challenged by *Hamlet*. Audience expectations are met in that *Hamlet* is recognized as a revenge tragedy, but they are thwarted by the way conventions are transformed. Most conspicuously, an audience is given an elaborate manifestation of Hamlet's psychological regeneration in a genre where degeneration is the norm.

Hamlet is a play about revenge against a regicide by a protagonist who is the patrilineal candidate for the throne, a situation paralleled only in academic renditions of the Orestes saga. The situation is complicated by the Danish "election" of their king, a process which seemingly consti-tutes an alternative to patrilineal succession. That complication is reduced, however, by the abridged society of the play. Claudius is a murderer, and, no mention of female succession being made, Hamlet is the only other noble of rank. Laertes' brief gesture of rebellion suggests a people capable of rising against the throne, but Laertes shares Polonius's view that under normal conditions the gap between the royal family and their own is unbreachable. No English audience would be likely to perceive Hamlet as a rebellious subject contemplating the (real or imagined) abuses of legitimately constituted authority, as would be the case with the avengers of such plays as *The Spanish Tragedy*, *The Revenger's Tragedy*, or *The Maid's Tragedy*. *Hamlet* excepted, only *The Malcontent*, a satiric comedy, casts a legitimate ruler in the role of avenger in the public theater.

In part, however, generic expectation overrides evaluation. Hamlet can play at being the ambitious subject; in his conversation with Rosencrantz and Guildenstern, this pose seems almost a validation of Claudius's usurpation. However, the play increasingly directs an audience to regard Hamlet as kingly by means of credible recognitions of his royalty. Thus, Horatio responds to Hamlet's narration of his triumphs at sea: "Why, what a king is this!" And Fortinbras affords him the funeral ceremonies appropriate to a warrior king.

> Let four captains
> Bear Hamlet like a soldier to the stage,
> For he was likely, had he been put on,
> To have prov'd most royal; and for his passage,
> The soldier's music and the rite of war
> Speak loudly for him.
>
> (V.ii.395–400)

Fortinbras establishes his own authority by ordering the disposition of the bodies, but the peal of ordnance that closes the play is for Hamlet. Hamlet's own dying advocacy of Fortinbras's election seems further to suggest the legitimacy of Hamlet's connection to the throne. The point is not that the character named Hamlet "is" the legitimate heir but that such claims are muted until Act V.

While the entire spectrum of revenge tragedy satisfies the loose Renaissance conception of tragedy, very little of it (perhaps only *Hamlet*) satisfies the humanist philosophical tradition which, by the twentieth century, makes tragedy a means of validation, as it is for Arthur Miller's Willie Loman and his ilk. (Revenge tragedy has two avenues of cultural reentry: the anthropological reinvestment in violence and the kind of canonization of decadence that follows in the wake of the French symbolists.) The privileging of tragedy as a philosophical stance in the humanist tradition has sufficiently overridden other considerations in our reception of *Hamlet* that it has become periodically necessary to reestablish that the play could not have been written to validate the avenger as avenger in the way that *Death of a Salesman* validates the common man.

Umberto Eco has suggested that "behind every strategy of the symbolic mode ... there is a legitimating theology."[7] This "theology" may be either secular or religious. Our cultural investment in Hamlet involves a symbolic reading of the character in whom we find the embodiment of the concerns of Western philosophy, even as that philosophy itself evolves. The authorizing theology is not difficult to find: it is humanism. And as humanism has evolved, so has Hamlet, from Renaissance to Romantic Hamlet, from Freudian to existentialist. If humanism has been eclipsed by post-modernist thought, the new theology preaches on the site of the old church (even in the midst of the deconstruction of its roof beams). My concern is not to pit authorizing theologies against each other but to examine the reasons for such an investment — to describe the textual strategies that invite these theologies.

E. D. Hirsch has discussed the role of genre in interpretation in a way which suggests an approach to *Hamlet*'s textual strategies. Hirsch insists that the validity of interpretation depends on the author's willed meaning, but one of the possible kinds of meaning is a willed type: "In some genres this willed meaning deliberately embraces analogous and unforeseeable implications."[8] Hirsch defines "intrinsic genre" as "that sense of the whole by means of which an interpreter can correctly understand any part in its determinacy."[9] "Intrinsic genre" is a more fluid concept than that of traditional literary genre, but it embraces such traditional uses of the term as denote the mutual expectations of author and audience. Such a rough untheorized genre as revenge tragedy fits this formulation nicely.

The question provoked by Hirsch's theory is this: can we reconcile the traditional openness of our reading of *Hamlet* with the assumption that revenge tragedy is the intrinsic genre of the play, the sense of the whole which allows us to understand the parts as we go along? The alternative is not in itself absurd. A traditional hermeneutics would read the play, reformulate a sense of its structure, and reread. Given some four hundred years and thousands of priestly readers, any primitive generic assumption would be obliterated. Or at least that would be the case were there not a periodic revival of primitive meaning. But the interpretive alternatives are not necessarily at odds. If the play makes use of those traits whereby it is recognized as revenge tragedy to problematize generic expectations, then we are directed toward openness rather than toward closure by those traits.

This problematization by means of generic traits is an efficient means of activating the symbolic mode as what Eco calls "a modality of textual use."[10] Eco's formulation of the term "symbolic" provides a means of validating an "open" reading of *Hamlet*. For Eco, the symbol is a textual element that is recognized as the projection of a content-nebula.[11] The recognition is provoked by a sense that rules have been violated.

> The textual implicature signaling the appearance of the symbolic mode depends on the presentation of a sentence, of a word, of an object, of an action that, according to the precoded narrative or discursive frames, to the acknowledged rhetorical rules, to the most common linguistic usages, *should not* have the relevance it acquires within that context.

Yet the interpreter believes that the violation did not occur "by chance or mistake" but signals a "*surplus* of signification."[12] It is not by a word or by a sentence that *Hamlet* provokes us to a symbolic reading but by a shift in emphasis from the action of revenge toward the self-definition of the subject who acts. Hamlet's range of thought is provocatively unspecific to the action of the play, and it is certainly not predicted by the precoded narrative frame of the revenge tragedy. A nebula of philosophical, psychological, and theological content surrounds his contemplation.

In Eco's theory of semiotics, the term content-nebula, deriving originally from Yuri Lotman, describes a state of not fully differentiated contents conveyed by expressive texts rather than by a highly articulated code.[13] Revenge tragedy in general undertakes a program which provides textual resolutions of the conflict between legal codes and the individual's sense of justice. (As Bowers suggests, the genre degenerates as it begins to evade this conflict.) But rather than resolving a conflict of two systems of codes in a textual narrative, *Hamlet* multiplies the number of conflicts, positing a protagonist who becomes aware of the inadequacy and incompatibility of all his articulated codes. The resolution of the play is a text (Hamlet's "story") embedded within a larger text (Providence) which is always unfolding before us.[14] To bring an argument full circle, the legitimating theology that authorizes a symbolic reading of the text does not simply seize on *Hamlet* as the arbitrary pretext for a humanist mystification. Rather, we find within a genre in the process of substituting texts for a grammar of codes, a text that signals its surplus signification by a significant redistribution of emphasis. The result of this redistribution is to extend the range of codes that are being replaced by the text. The legitimating theology implied by the conclusion of *Hamlet* is that Renaissance Christian humanism which undertakes to read the world as God's book. In its broadest implications the theology underlies all Renaissance inquiry, but we need not posit such a modern philosophical overview for the London theater audience. England saw the hand of Providence in its own history: in the defeat of the Armada, in the very dynastic struggles that Shakespeare staged in his history plays. In very practical terms, narrative was viewed as significant.

Like its protagonist, *Hamlet* argues that "There are more things in heaven and earth … [t]han are dreamt of in your philosophy." Implicitly the play substitutes narrative for philosophical discourse. So long as an authorizing theology continues to accord significance to narrative — that is, to assert that there are things to be said in books that cannot be said in handbooks — a continuous symbolic use of the text can be sustained. A narrative may survive the recodification of experience because it was never reconciled with the old codification. The symbolic mode may be undermined, however, by the devaluation of experience. Richard Schechner's essay, "The End of Humanism," correlates the emergence of postmodernism with such a devaluation of both narrative and experience. [15] Such a philosophical shift creates a radical discontinuity in the "authorizing theology" and calls into question the symbolic use of the text.

We need not in fact wait for postmodernism to see such a devaluation of experience. One aspect of the narrative degeneration that we find in *Der Bestrafte Brudermord*, the mid-seventeenth-century German version of *Hamlet* (preserved in an eighteenth-century text), is the explanation of narrative in terms of rule. Hamlet's encounter with Claudius at prayer, a textual conundrum in Shakespeare, becomes in the German variant simply a search for the correct rule.

> I have been following the cursed dog so long, and
> I have found him alone at last. Now is the time to take his life,
> while he is alone and in the midst of his most earnest

> devotions. [*Moves to stab him*.] But no! I shall let him
> finish his prayer. But oh! now I think of it, he did not
> give my father time to say his prayers but sent him with
> his sins, while asleep, perhaps to hell. Therefore I shall
> send him along to the same place. [*Again moves to stab
> him from behind*.] But pause, Hamlet! Why do you wish
> to take his sins upon yourself? I shall permit him to say
> his prayer, and I shall now depart, granting him his life.
> But at another time I shall surely exact my revenge.
>
> (III.ii.1–12)[16]

In the closet scene of *Der Bestrafte Brudermord*, the Queen views the situation in Denmark as a chain of events ultimately due to the failure to enforce a simple rule.

> Oh heavens, to what excess of frenzy has
> this Prince's melancholy driven him! Ah, my only Prince
> has entirely lost his wits. If I had not taken in marriage
> my brother-in-law, my former husband's brother, I
> would not have maneuvered the crown of Denmark
> out of my son's grasp. But what can one do about things
> already done? Nothing. Things must remain as they are.
> If the Pope had forbidden me such a marriage, this
> would never have happened. I shall go and take most
> careful thought, how I may help my son to regain his
> former sanity and health.
>
> (III.vi.14–24)

As diminishments of the Shakespearean text, these speeches invite our laughter, but they are not inherently illogical. Rather, it is their imperturbable rationalism that devalues experience and reduces the signification of the narrative.

The conventional response of an audience watching a play is determined by its response to conventional signals along the way rather than by the revelation of the play's ultimate logical form, even though form may dominate both artistic conception and critical response.[17] For revenge tragedy, atmospheric expectations are far more consistent than the ethical framework. No play more fully illustrates the consequences of private revenge than *Romeo and Juliet*, but revenge in the play is neither covert nor delayed, and the atmosphere of the play avoids the macabre.

Chettle's *Hoffman* generates the appeal of a revenge drama without raising serious ethical issues: the offense against the protagonist is the legal execution of his father for piracy.

The most emotionally compelling feature of the revenge tragedy and its progeny is the association of revenge with macabre ceremony. The source of this ceremony was a Senecan heritage seasoned with accounts of Continental treachery and stimulated, no doubt, by the normal atrocities of public criminal justice. Hieronymo's murderous drama, Vindice's scenario with a poisoned skull, Bosola's staging of waxen images of the dead, and Titus Andronicus's cannibalistic banquet are among the better known of such ceremonies and suggest a sustained taste for this sort of incivility. In *Hamlet*, the macabre and the perverse are displaced from the protagonist, but the fundamental transgression of the boundary between the living and the dead is preserved.

In part, the ghost becomes the vehicle of the macabre. The ghost of Hamlet's father bridges two worlds, hinting at the torments of a world beyond (or between) but remaining emotionally linked not only to his murderer but to his wife. Hamlet's ambivalent response to the ghost reflects the problematic nature of this border straddling: Hamlet is both moved by his father's suffering and fearful of diabolical temptation. Critics are, on the whole, kind to the ghost, though Prosser most notably labels him an agent of evil. Nonetheless, the dramatic effectiveness of Shakespeare's ghost is worth emphasizing. We need only compare his effect on the play with that of such pallid rivals as the ghost in Kyd's *Spanish Tragedy*, who spends his time conversing with Revenge, an abstract personification of the action, or that of the ghost in *The Atheist's Tragedy*, who would "leave revenge unto the King of kings" (II.vi.22), a theologically sound but dramatically deadly proposition. [18]

A far more frequent connection to the world of the dead than the ghostly visitation is the preservation of the bodies of the dead (in whole or in parts). Hieronymo preserves his son's body, Vindice his lover's skull. The bodies of the dead may be used to torment the living, as in *Titus Andronicus,* or as in *The Duchess of Malfi,* where a self-conscious variation substitutes waxen bodies in a variation on a theme — a variation supposing a norm of atrocity. An alternative variation occurs in *The Atheist's Tragedy,* where a man thought to be dead rises up to disrupt a rape attempt in a charnel house.

The impulse to mingle with the dead is rendered less grotesquely in

Hamlet's extensive graveyard scene. Earlier in the play, Hamlet's mockery of the dead Polonius and his subsequent concealment of the body involve the protagonist in some of the unnatural treatment of the dead that we expect in revenge tragedy, but the play moves to a more philosophical attitude toward mortality. Hamlet's grappling with Laertes at Ophelia's grave site may constitute a violation of the normal standards of social decorum, but by the standards of revenge tragedy the gesture is mild. In this action, Hamlet may even be seen to object to the mingling with the dead seen in Laertes' leap into Ophelia's grave. The most recognizable iconic image in the play is that of Hamlet contemplating the skull of Yorick. It is a commonplace that this skull becomes a *memento mori* in the medieval tradition, but the context of revenge tragedy suggests that we might find conspicuous the absence of perversity both in the manner and in the occasion of his coming in contact with it. The grave digger displaces the bones of the dead for a new grave. Regardless of whatever phobias about such displacement Shakespeare's own gravestone may reveal, the touch is naturalistic, not macabre. Yorick's skull provides Hamlet with an opportunity to contemplate death in its normal course — an opportunity not generally afforded in revenge tragedy — and to express loss in terms far less hyperbolic than those which violent death would generate.

　　The most flamboyant excesses of revenge tragedy occur subsequent to *Hamlet* in plays of seemingly self-conscious decadence. At some point, the naive violence of *The Spanish Tragedy*, Shakespeare's own *Titus Andronicus*, and perhaps even that most celebrated of hypothetical objects, the *Ur-Hamlet*, left two directions for development: the enlistment of consciousness in the service of violence, which produces the Jacobean extravaganzas, or the reaction of consciousness against violence, which works against the grain of the genre.

　　Hamlet breaks with the ceremony of revenge that commonly dehumanizes the revenger-protagonist. It has hardly gone unnoticed that Hamlet makes no plans that would control the manner in which he avenges himself on Claudius. He plots no cannibalistic banquet, murderous court entertainment, or tryst with the dead for his antagonist. Nevertheless, the perversion of norms which such revenge rituals would imply pervades the pattern of violated ceremony which Bevington observes in the play. In Bevington's formulation, Hamlet retreats from the "fulsomely ceremonial royal presence" of Claudius, repelled, even before the ghost's revelation, by the unnatural displacement of ceremonies of grief by ceremonies of conjugal joy.[19] Fergusson's classic study analyses the play as "a species of ritual drama" whose progress may best be seen as a series of rituals.[20] It is clear that the perverted ritual is central to *Hamlet* and that the effect of that ritual is to show a fundamental disruption of order, but it is equally clear that the protagonist, by a series of careful displacements, is distanced from any role as the celebrant of satanic ceremonies.

In the saga that is the ultimate source for *Hamlet*, Amleth's means of revenge becomes a riddle with which he confronts the King.[21] His wooden stakes, Amleth's spears, become the instruments by means of which he traps the King and his defenders beneath the knitted hangings of the royal hall and burns them alive. One may suppose that no man has the impulse to depict fire in a wooden theater, but Hamlet's tacit refusal to revel in the contemplation of any specific means of revenge is an important element in preventing his dehumanization. The major rituals in which Hamlet is involved — the Mousetrap play and the fencing match — evoke the atmosphere requisite for revenge tragedy but absolve him of any imputation of the satanic.

In the Mousetrap play, we may see Hieronymo's bloody ceremony reduced to psychological assault. In Hieronymo's play, fictional murders are enacted in reality; in Hamlet's, the real murder of King Hamlet is represented in fiction. The real and the fictional are entwined in both cases, but the moral positions of the two producers are radically different. In the aftermath of his ceremony, Hamlet revels in the emotions of the avenger: he could "drink hot blood." Yet Hamlet quotes the avenger rather than becoming one. In stabbing the eavesdropping Polonius, Hamlet even claims a victim. But the ceremony, the words, and the act are separated, and responsibility is dissipated.

The climactic fencing match provides a macabre ceremony, but again the play diverts blame from the protagonist. The poisoned sword and chalice become the instruments of Hamlet's revenge, but they are provided by the King's plot, not his own. Hamlet's participation in the fencing match follows the forms appropriate to the duel, and he manifests all the skills necessary to win a single combat with Laertes, but he enters the match without the intention of taking Laertes' life. Whatever honor accrues to the duel, he achieves; whatever dishonor, he avoids by his ignorance of the plot. The scene becomes a shambles. Hamlet's twofold slaying of Claudius by poisoned sword and cup has all the savage irony of the revenge tragedy, but none of its sustained intentionality. That the Queen dies at the hand of the man who murdered to marry her constitutes both an expected repercussion of the strategy of violence and a kind of redemption for Gertrude. Knowingly or not, she drinks the poison intended for her son. Even Laertes, a more thoughtless avenger than Hamlet, undertakes his task somewhat reluctantly, impelled by the mechanics of honor but repelled by the underhandedness of his own means. If we begin with the norms of social ceremony, then we find in the play a perversion of those norms. If we begin with the conventions of revenge tragedy, in which the protagonist contrives a ceremony that both destroys his adversary and embeds the avenger himself in rituals of lawlessness, then we find in the play a rectification of the protagonist's action that allows him to avoid psychological degeneration. Hamlet is not innocent in terms of the moral norms of Elizabethan England, nor does revenge tragedy in general suggest that those norms be suspended. The movement of the play against the grain of theatrical expectations creates in the audience a psychological sense of Hamlet's innocence rather than a legalistic one, and makes possible the traditional perception of his psychological recuperation in Act V.

We are left with one characteristic of revenge tragedy that is fore-grounded rather than evaded. The protagonist's action is a reaction. The revenge tragedy begins with the momentum of prior events (or must take time for a cumbersome double movement). This momentum of events serves to undermine the Aristotelian framework of analysis imposed by the critical and literary tradition that developed Aristotle's formulation. We look for the *hamartia*, the missing of the mark, but a descent has already begun. In Shakespeare's other great tragedies — *Macbeth*, *Othello*, and *Lear* — the choice not taken could have avoided fatality. In *Hamlet*, the choice not taken, or not taken quickly, is the choice to kill. This is anomalous in itself, although we may argue that most societies, and certainly Elizabethan society and our own are numbered among them, legitimize, even require, the taking of human life under conditions that each society specifies. The play clearly sanctions the killing of Claudius when it occurs. What fascinates us about the event is not whether the killing is ethical but whether it is a choice.

Hamlet returns from Wittenberg to lament, "The time is out of joint — O cursed spite, / That ever I was born to set it right!" If he returned today, he would complain, "I've just arrived, but I find myself always already inscribed." And if being laden with the Name of the Father (*nom du père, non du père*) isn't sufficient burden, Hamlet finds himself reenveloped by Claudius, within the family, within the body of Denmark. It is his struggle against this incorporation which generates his assault on the social order and on language itself. Though it is by no means a sufficient explanation of Hamlet's recuperation, his expulsion from Denmark is a natural correlative to his renewal.

It has seemed to such critics as Barker that the revolutionary Hamlet of Acts I-IV is replaced by an instrument of duty in Act V.[22] Certainly in an English context, Hamlet's reconciliation with Providence would imply a thorough reconciliation with social order. But without that context, the results are less certain. The King who invokes divinity as his hedge is soon dead. The Hamlet of Act IV equates power with excrement, if we can so construe his observation that "a king may go a progress through the guts of a beggar." The postrevolutionary Hamlet of Act V still imagines "the noble dust of Alexander ... stopping a bunghole" — the tap hole of a beer barrel, of course, but not without unsavory connotations as well.

If Hamlet's language is less challenging in Act V, it is perhaps because he learns there is no "talking cure" for his dilemma. There is perhaps a water cure, the sea voyage, whose immediate and extraneous dangers disrupt the momentum of the past events that burden Hamlet, as they burden any avenger. But on his return, he does not array himself, like Prince Hal become King Henry, in the full armor of social rhetoric. Hamlet's "interim" between necessities is not, like Hal's "holiday," a measure of time excluded, or bracketed, from the definition of a social self. Without an English context to override the questions implicit in the dramatic context, issues are not resolved by placing power in the right hands and leaving the apparatus of power intact. In the mayhem of its closure, *Hamlet* offers no such false certainty. Overridden (and overwritten) by history, tragedy becomes a retrospective rather than a prospective art. Had Eliot not been a retrospective thinker, he might have said, "There can be no *English* tragedy."

The combination of genres that might be described as hybridization in a comparatively thorough and theoretized theatrical project like tragicomedy, occurs as incursion, juxtaposition, or even collision in more haphazard cases. In the most mixed of the Elizabethan plays, generic components combine in ways we might better describe as plate tectonics than architectonics because cultural responses to these components will vary at differing rates while a culture nonetheless remains continually committed to the conceptual unity of the whole. Thus, we struggle with the relationship of Hal and Falstaff, or perhaps we make Mercutio the hero of *Romeo and Juliet*. Changing cultural responses may be evolutionary or revolutionary, may deconstruct or reconstruct, but they will not be exerted on a rigid structure. The provenance of the stories underlying English revenge tragedies deracinates their characters. Because these characters have no mythic significance for England, the dynastic implications of Greek tragedy are precluded, and a greater burden is placed on the action. That the plots of novellas enjoyed greater popularity as sources than classic myths argues that a certain measure of satisfaction might have derived from the xenophobic pleasure of watching Continental scenes of mayhem. Such base pleasures, so like our culture's base pleasure in the vengeance film, work against the cathartic effect of Aristotelian tragedy, inciting perhaps fascination and fear, but not pity. The favorite setting for revenge tragedy, Italy, offers a confused welter of city-state nobles, important enough for power politics but not sufficient to evoke the divinity that hedges a king. Whatever instability in settings like France or Spain might be implied by the lawlessness of revenge tragedy was similarly unlikely to alarm an Elizabethan.

Although *Hamlet* consistently evokes the atmospheric traits of these revenge tragedies, its fundamental logic is otherwise derived.[23] The source of *Hamlet*, insofar as we find it in *Historiae Danicae*, is saga, more deeply rooted in mythic thinking than the novella. The saga hero Amleth succeeds by the laws of folklore rather by those of Machiavellian intrigue. In folklore, the fool is habitually wise, and the disinherited inherit. Amleth's only defense against a deadly enemy is his pretense of idiocy, but the combat takes place through ritual tests and riddling responses with ramifications that exceed the needs of immediate strategy.

Amleth is a truth sayer. Attempts to determine his mental competence are met with responses that are simultaneously sense and nonsense. Told by his companions that a wolf that has crossed his path is a young colt, Amleth wishes more such colts in his stepfather's stable: his nonsense becomes a curse. The primary test of his competence is sexual temptation, normal sexual response being regarded as proof of his sanity. He contrives to lie with a young woman and to boast of it, but, having placed beneath his bed fragments of a coxcomb, a hoof, and a ceiling, he is able to claim that he has performed the act in what are construed as preposterous places. The hero thus preserves life, potency, and truth. The saga's chief riddle is Amleth's spears, the wooden crooks that he hardens in the King's fire in plain sight and that he ultimately uses to trap the King beneath his tapestries in order to wreak vengeance on him. Significantly, the truth is as important to Amleth as the deception.

Amleth's truth saying is more than mere cunning: it is mixed with a touch of prophecy. On Amleth's trip to Britain (as in *Hamlet*, the trip is a scheme to destroy the Danish King's young adversary), he insult's Britain's King, the Queen, and members of the banquet feast with seeming riddles that discover the truth that the King's father was a slave, that the Queen's mother was a bondmaid, and that the food is tainted with blood. Though Amleth's adventures in Britain never enter *Hamlet*, we find in the primitive figure the same uncanny capacity for truth that characterizes Shakespeare's protagonist. Hamlet's mad conversation is more discursive than the idiot riddles that form the core of Amleth's wisdom, but Hamlet similarly dares the hearer to face the truth about himself. Madness on the Elizabethan stage serves purposes similar to those of idiocy in folklore. As Robert Weimann observes, madness is not only an object of representation but a mode of representation.[24]

Much that characterizes Amleth is left behind as he becomes Hamlet, but the civilized version retains a mythic aura that no Elizabethan avenger shares. His prophetic soul divines his uncle's evil; he senses the danger in the King's message to England; he feels the imminent crisis before the fencing match with Laertes. There is a perfect logic to his suspicions, of course, but our attention is drawn to his intuitive capacities. Unlike the hero of folktale, however, he hesitates to credit his own intuition.

The setting, Denmark, also retains something of its primitive character. Without a tradition of its own on the Elizabethan stage, Denmark is nonetheless contrasted with Paris, a source of sophistication for Laertes, and Wittenberg, a source of intellectual training for Hamlet. Until the appearance of Osric suggests a direction in which Denmark is drifting, the Danes are defined as a nation of martial character with only one characteristic vice, the inclination to drink. Conspicuously absent are the array of sexual profligates that populate the typical revenge tragedy, particularly in its decadence. In the plays of Chapman, Marston, Webster, and Tourneur, unprincipled fornication is the norm. In *Hamlet* the hidden evil lies beneath a surface sufficiently austere that the Prince's satire seems artificially imported to the world of the play. Or at least it seems so if we ignore theatrical fashion.

The association of satire and revenge results in part from their coincidental rise in popularity, but they are natural companions. Both revenge and satire challenge the order of things as they are. Arguably, the protagonist of Marston's *Malcontent*, a satiric comedy, influenced the development of the avenger as much as did any tragic protagonist of the period.[25] Marston's *Antonio's Revenge* is a relentlessly bloodthirsty spectacle intended to be performed by child actors. Debate cannot resolve whether it is a parody of the revenge genre or merely a heavy-handed example. Middleton alternated between city comedy and revenge tragedy based on similarly corrupt worlds. Webster's Bosola is a malcontent turned to villainous purposes who nonetheless justifies himself with a satirist's moral message. As a result of the tendency of satire and revenge tragedy to meld on the Elizabethan stage, the characters in revenge tragedy are often pervasively corrupt. But though their corruption may be thematically related to the primary crimes in these plays, it is not part of the chain of causality.

Hamlet acknowledges the vogue for satire without being subsumed by it. Hamlet reads, or pretends to read, a satire on old men and belabors Polonius with its contents. Furthermore, he tends to the conventional in his denunciation of women's wiles to Ophelia; in truth, women's cosmetics and techniques of flirtation have little to do with his reasons for distrusting her or his mother. Perhaps his speech to Ophelia smacks of the satirist's cliches because he expects to be overheard, but no such consideration influences him in the graveyard when he envisions Yorick's skull as a messenger to ladies who must come to its condition though they paint an inch thick. Hamlet remains a satirist once removed. Conscious of his role, he is struck not by his own wit but by the astonishing truth of satiric commonplaces. He tells Ophelia that beauty subverts honesty: such a conflict "was sometime a paradox," an exercise in sophistry to amuse young wits, "but the time gives it proof."

The characters in *Hamlet* are not particularly well suited to satire. With the exception of Osric, whose faults never become crimes, they never pursue any wrongdoing except at the instigation of the King. Polonius does nothing that would be contemptible in the service of a good king, and his foolishness is a reasonably amiable loss of focus rather than a substantial misunderstanding of the behavior appropriate to his age. He is, we traditionally assume, unduly suspicious of Hamlet's intentions toward his daughter and mildly unscrupulous in his supervision of his son's behavior. But if he is excessively concerned with reputation, there is no hidden misbehavior of his own to make him seem hypocritical. That Ophelia obeys her father is hardly a conventional vice. She becomes Hamlet's tool, through his pretense of madness, before she is used against him by Polonius and Claudius. Laertes is plausibly impassioned by the loss of both remaining members of his family, and yet still has half a mind to forgive Hamlet. Rosencrantz and Guildenstern, "the indifferent children of the earth," are easily misdirected, but they are bywords for mediocrity, not depravity. The Queen's moral responsibility derives from the central action of the play and is not a habitual vice.

The clearest indicator of how these characters might have been portrayed differently is provided by Shakespeare's own *Troilus and Cressida*, the play in which he is most influenced by satiric drama, written perhaps a year after *Hamlet*. There vices proliferate. Pandarus peddles, Cressida falls, Diomedes seduces, Ajax fumes, Achilles sulks, Thersites rails. Those with the vision to see the immorality of this world, Hector and Ulysses, nonetheless serve it. By focusing on social disorder, satire typically undermines the metaphysical implications of tragedy as a genre. By systematically circumscribing the satiric elements of *Hamlet*, Shakespeare allows scope to the mythic elements of the play.

The classic comparison of Hamlet and Orestes by Gilbert Murray uncovered striking similarities not only in the structure of the myths involving the two figures but in the way those myths evolved from their earliest narrative formulations to dramatic form. Each protagonist must act against the kinsman who has displaced his father and against his own mother. Each returns to the place of his birth as a stranger and undertakes a guarded assault on the throne. In the dramatic versions of the two stories, the mental distress of the heroes becomes central. Further examination of both stories suggested to Murray that underlying them was the myth of the alternation of the gods of summer and winter, the conjecture that became central to almost all reading of myth in the era of *The Golden Bough*. Murray's comparison is most interesting, however, not in determining the mythic common denominator but in noting how the

narrative is problematized at the point at which mythic agents are viewed
as both conscious of their roles and psychologically comprehensible to an
audience. Such an audience will accept, even expect, extraordinary
actions, but it will also expect normal emotional reactions.[26]

The key tension in dramatized myth is that its plot has been established by a narrative that had no need to consider the motivations of the
characters. Characters in myth represent collective, or abstract, actions,
not those of an individual. Ascribing individual consciousness to mythic
behavior is likely to produce puzzling incongruities, particularly if the
original myth is not still culturally active. Myths of origin, for example,
frequently involve actions, like incest, that are considered primary taboos
in the evolved society which continues to preserve the mythic narrative.
Collective values do not always parallel individual values: murder is
shameful, but war is epic; theft is shameful, but conquest is glorious.
Almost any myth is subject to some *reducio ad absurdum* which will
demonstrate that the characters involved do not meet the moral, or even
the intellectual standards, of the society that engenders them. We are
accustomed to reading myth without such simplification. We trust the
implicit value judgments of a mythic narrative if we trust the values of
the society it represents. Conversely, if we distrust those values, we look
for some duplicity in the myth structure that underlies them and lends
them ideological support. The process of dramatizing a myth creates two
opportunities for challenging its values. The playwright may explicitly
examine the values implied by the received narrative, or the dramatic
genre may implicitly question the values of the source through its intrinsic value system.

The values of Elizabethan England mount a confused assault on the
assumptions of the Amleth myth. The worldview of the Renaissance
Christian is fitfully applied to the events of *Hamlet* in a manner that
seems largely parenthetical. Hamlet speaks of suicide, for example, first
in a Christian manner, obeying God's "canon 'gainst self-slaughter."
Then he speaks in an agnostic manner in which he yields to fear of "what
dreams may come." Ophelia's suicide, under conditions of reduced
mental capacity, is discussed in terms of ecclesiastical legalism. Horatio,
however, perhaps aptly Roman in name, avoids the Roman solution to
the emptiness of life not because suicide would bar him from felicity but
because he must tell Hamlet's story.

By invoking Christian values, the play reminds the audience (particularly the original audience) that its value system is not consistently compatible with that of characters in the play, but the play does not create a model of how such values as the revenge ethic would specifically affect the conscience of a Christian. Rather, it creates an abstract model of how the mind reacts to value conflicts and abhorrent alternatives. The ethical status of revenge is never actually debated. Instead, the juxtaposition of Christian theology and the dynamics of the plot creates ambiguous evidence concerning the moral status of both Hamlet and his father's spirit. When Claudius finds himself unable to cleanse his conscience because he cannot repent, his analysis of his spiritual state is straightforward and the audience accepts it. When Hamlet refuses to kill Claudius because he fears to send a praying King to Heaven, the case is less clear. It is evident that attempting to damn the King would be diabolical. But in refraining from killing the King because he might be caught in a more typical spiritual condition on some unspecified future occasion, Hamlet contemplates a sin but does not commit one. The ghost, I would suggest, is primarily a dramatic ghost, operating in the same kind of theological gray area that suicide occupies in the play. In his attitude to Claudius, he may be construed as either a pagan or a diabolical ghost: he demands retribution. In his continued love for his wife, he seems Christian. He both warns Hamlet against violence toward her during his appearance on the battlements and counsels Hamlet in how to ease her conscience during the closet scene. Like the dream ghosts of Bosworth field, Hamlet Senior continues to interest himself in the world in a worldly way, but nonetheless in a way that ultimately furthers the well-being of the state. In the final analysis, the play's explicit formulations of ethical issues are relatively insignificant.

The transition from epic saga to tragedy profoundly challenges the values of the original.[27] Victory predominates in epic, suffering in tragedy. Amleth triumphs over Feng in the saga as a reward for his endurance and resourcefulness. Similarly, Orestes in *The Odyssey* stands as an example to Telemachus of filial duty and valor. Dramatic form shifts the emphasis to the suffering of these agents. Though the matter of epic may be suited to dramatic narrative, the perspective will change. Revenge is of central importance to epic. To cite two conspicuous examples, both *The Iliad* and *The Odyssey* culminate in successful acts of revenge. If the revenge agent is a tragic protagonist, however, and the revenge itself is in any sense a purgation, then the protagonist's death must contribute to the sense of purgation or be irrelevant to what the play is about. The relation of the protagonist's suffering to his aggressive action is either deeply rooted in the structure of a revenge play or the play moves away from tragic form.

In *The Oresteia*, Orestes' persecution by the Furies ultimately precipitates Athena's decision to invite the Furies, as the Eumenides, into a relationship with the city of Athens, an act that both acknowledges them and dilutes their influence. *Hamlet* cannot be described in comparable cultural terms. The Prince achieves a kingship in death; his story continues in the world; and his potential value as King remains unsullied by the bloodshed. A dynasty is felt to conclude with his potential kingship rather than with Claudius's usurpation. These events resolve the plot but conspicuously do not resolve the underlying conflict of codes. Unlike *The Oresteia*, *Hamlet* does not represent a final stage of cultural revision. The dynastic struggles of Denmark play no part in England's national mythology. This very disconnectedness frees the play from history and allows it a phenomenological argument, which is nonetheless free to encounter history again and again.

Notes

Introduction

1. The power of the bare stage has found its most eloquent spokesman in Peter Brook. See Peter Brook, *The Empty Space* (New York: Atheneum, 1978).
2. See, in particular, Marvin Rosenberg, *The Masks of Hamlet* (Newark: University of Delaware Press, 1992). See also John L. Styan, *The Shakespeare Revolution* (Cambridge: Cambridge University Press, 1977). As an introduction, see Michael Goldman, *The Actor's Freedom: Toward a Theory of Drama* (New York: Viking, 1975).
3. M. Merleau-Ponty, *Phenomenology of Perception*, trans. Colin Smith (New York: Humanities University Press, 1962).
4. Stephen Greenblatt, *Shakespearean Negotiations: The Circulation of Social Energy in Renaissance England* (Berkeley: University of California Press, 1988), 1–20.

Chapter 1. Space and Scrutiny in *Hamlet*

1. See Susanne K. Langer, *Feeling and Form* (New York: Scribner, 1953). Langer views drama as "virtual history in the mode of dramatic action" and distinguishes it from pure literature (306–25). See John L. Styan, "Stage Space and the Shakespeare Experience," in *Shakespeare and the Sense of Performance*, ed. Marvin and Ruth Thompson (Newark: University of Delaware Press, 1989), 195–209. Styan examines the relationship of stage space to intimacy with the audience, distinguishing between "the space that joins" and "the space that divides" (211).
2. See Patrice Pavis, *Languages of the Stage: Essays in the Semiology of Theatre* (New York: Performing Arts Journal Publications, 1982). The onstage-offstage distinction together with the distinction between interior and exterior space constitute for Pavis major textual distinctions that performance must respect (156).

3. See Harry Berger, Jr., "Text against Performance in Shakespeare: The Example of *MacBeth*," *Genre* 7 (1982): 49–79. Berger argues that in close analysis text supersedes performance. I argue that stage parameters directly generated by the text may be examined with equal rigor.

4. See Maynard Mack, "The World of *Hamlet*," *The Yale Review* 41 (1952): 502–23. In his classic essay, Mack observes the interrogative mood of the rhetoric of the play.

5. See James L. Calderwood, *To Be and Not To Be: Negation and Metadrama in* Hamlet (New York: Columbia University Press, 1983). Calderwood extensively explores verbal negation in *Hamlet*.

6. See Walter N. King, *Hamlet's Search for Meaning* (Athens: University of Georgia Press, 1982). King examines Hamlet's quest in terms of Christian existentialism.

7   See Fredson Bowers, *Elizabethan Revenge Tragedy* (Princeton: Princeton University Press, 1940). Bowers thoroughly surveys the ethical wasteland of revenge tragedy.

8. See J. Dover Wilson, *What Happens in* Hamlet, 3rd ed. (Cambridge: Cambridge University Press, 1951). Wilson's argument, dating from 1935, is that a more perceptive Claudius must be distracted during the Mousetrap (137–98).

9. Almost any discussion of the ghost, short of a book-length study, oversimplifies him. He appears for an extensive period of time in Act I; he appears briefly in Act IV; and then he disappears. His disappearance is his most benevolent act. Hamlet is clearly horrified by his presence, and the culturally based distrust of him detailed by Eleanor Prosser in Hamlet *and Revenge* (Stanford, Calif.: Stanford University Press, 1967) is a significant factor in our viewing of the play. Yet to see in his intervention in the closet a diabolical delicacy which prevents Gertrude's true repentance by evoking maternal protectiveness (195–98) is to inquire too curiously: damnation and the maternal instinct make strange bedfellows in the Elizabethan cultural context or our own.

10. Experimental drama that reapproaches pure ritual may involve these senses as religious ceremony does regularly, but in so doing it eliminates any absolute distinction between actor and spectator. Certain odors may emanate from the stage — the smell of incense or gunpowder, for example — but no consistent control of such effects has yet occurred.

11. See Walter J. Ong, S.J., *Ramus, Method, and the Decay of Dialogue* (Cambridge: Harvard University Press, 1958), 270–318. The process by which the ghost's "voice" is transformed to the visual display of the Mousetrap play parallels the Renaissance movement away from voice that Ong attributes in part to the influence of Ramist rhetoric.

12. See Caroline F.E. Spurgeon, *Shakespeare's Imagery and What It Tells Us* (Cambridge: Cambridge University Press, 1935). Spurgeon makes the first detailed observation of the disease imagery that serves as poetic expression of the hidden evil. See Maurice Charney, *Style in* Hamlet

(Princeton: Princeton University Press, 1969). Charney gives more prominence to images of war. In terms of the actions of the play, I view martial impulses as consistently frustrated. In the main, Charney does not concern himself with the ironic effect of context.

13. See Alexandre Koyré, *From the Closed World to the Infinite Universe* (Baltimore: Johns Hopkins University Press, 1957), 28–57.

14. Merleau-Ponty, *Phenomenology of Perception*, 283–84.

15. Ibid., 284.

16. Rudolf Arnheim, *The Power of the Center: A Study of Composition in the Visual Arts,* rev. ed. (Berkeley: University of California Press, 1982).

17. See Sidney Homan, *Shakespeare's Theater of Presence: Language, Spectacle, and the Audience* (Lewisburg, Pa.: Bucknell University Press, 1989). Homan, speaking of Peter Shaffer's *Black Comedy*, notes that the representation of darkness becomes, inversely, a celebration of vision.

18. See Alan C. Dessen, *Elizabethan Drama and the Viewer's Eye* (Chapel Hill: University of North Carolina Press, 1977). Dessen explores the emblematic potential of Elizabethan stage properties (71–109).

19. See Norman Rabkin, *Shakespeare and the Common Understanding* (Chicago: University of Chicago Press, 1967). See also Francis Barker, *The Tremulous Private Body: Essays on Subjection* (London: Methuen, 1984).

20. See Pavis, *Languages of the Stage,* for an approach (somewhat favoring semiology) to a sorting out of the tasks of textual and performance analysis.

Chapter 2. Taking Up the Past: *Hamlet* and Time

1. See Robert Hapgood, "*Hamlet* Nearly Absurd: The Dramaturgy of Delay," *Tulane Drama Review* 9 (1965): 132–45. Hapgood discusses *Hamlet* in terms of drama of the absurd.

2. See Ricardo J. Quinones, *The Renaissance Discovery of Time* (Cambridge: Harvard University Press, 1972). Quinones evaluates Renaissance frameworks for time.

3. See Wylie Sypher, *The Ethic of Time: Structures of Experience in Shakespeare* (New York: Seabury, 1976). Sypher deals extensively with lived time, exploring both Renaissance concepts of time and those of modern philosophy (65–89). He argues that Hamlet ultimately accepts the moment without regard to past or future, a result which seems to me to dissociate Hamlet from his own life.

4. Henri Bergson, *Time and Free Will,* trans. F. L. Pogson, 4th ed. (New York: Macmillan, 1921). Bergson establishes the distinction and explores the implications for consciousness.

5. See Merleau-Ponty, *Phenomenology of Perception* for such a critique (415).
6. David Scott Kastan, *Shakespeare and the Shapes of Time* (Hanover, N.H.: University Press of New England, 1982).
7. John Webster, *The White Devil*, vol. 1 of *Jacobean Drama: An Anthology*, ed. Richard C. Harrier (1963; New York: Norton, 1968).
8. Charney, *Style in* Hamlet; Bernard Beckerman, *Dynamics of Drama: Theory and Method of Analysis* (1970; New York: Drama Book Specialists, 1979). See Charney (208) and Beckerman (194–95) for discussions of these mechanisms of interruption.
9. See Keir Elam, *The Semiotics of Theatre and Drama* (London: Methuen, 1980). Elam places the Russian theories in a theatrical context (119–20).
10. Langer, *Feeling and Form*. For her full development of the idea, see 306–66.
11. Herbert Blau, *Blooded Thought: Occasions of Theatre* (New York: Performing Arts Journal, 1982).
12. Stephen Booth, "On the Value of *Hamlet*," in *Reinterpretations of Elizabethan Drama: Selected Papers From the English Institute*, ed. Norman Rabkin (New York: Columbia University Press, 1969), 137–76.
13. Harley Granville-Barker, *Prefaces to Shakespeare*, vol. 1 (Princeton: Princeton University Press, 1946). Granville-Barker's justification of the divisions is essentially inextricable from his reading of the play (24–260).
14. Booth, King Lear, Macbeth, *Indefinition and Tragedy* (New Haven: Yale University Press, 1983). See Booth's reading of Macbeth's "Tomorrow, and tomorrow, and tomorrow," in which he demonstrates the rhetorical fusion of time past with time future (95). In rough terms we might see *Hamlet* as trailing behind it a shadow *Macbeth* which has imploded time before the play has begun.
15. William Shakespeare, *A New Variorum Edition of Shakespeare: Hamlet*, 4th ed., 3 vols., ed. H. H. Furness (Philadelphia: Lippencott, 1877), vol. 1. See Preface, xiv-xvii, for a detailed discussion of Shakespeare's double time scheme. See also nn. 391–94 for the debate on Hamlet's age, which we have yet to leave behind.
16. A few key studies may suggest the influence of psychological criticism. See Ernest Jones, *Hamlet and Oedipus* (1949; New York: Norton, 1976). Jones, in an argument first published in 1910, establishes the Oedipal reading. Although for Jones Hamlet should be in his late twenties, the issue of sexual confusion has suggested adolescence to theatrical practitioners. See Erik H. Erikson, *Identity: Youth and Crisis* (New York: Norton, 1968). Erikson focuses on Hamlet's value formation, fixing his age in the mid-twenties. See Anna K. Nardo, "Hamlet, 'A Man to Double Business Bound,'" *Shakespeare Quarterly* 34 (1983): 181–89. Nardo derives her model from Gregory Bateson's studies of the double-bind in disturbed children. Regardless of the age a psychological approach chooses for Hamlet, the tendency is to see his problem as arrested development. A more generalized anthropological view of rites of passage

for the individual in Renaissance society, focusing less narrowly on the adolescent, is that of Marjorie Garber, *Coming of Age in Shakespeare* (New York: Methuen, 1981).

17. See, for example, Prosser, Hamlet *and Revenge*, 144–45. The argument seems necessary to critics who "debunk" mainstream readings of the play. See Bernard Grebanier, *The Heart of* Hamlet (New York: Crowell, 1960). Grebanier argues that "the time element is of no consequence to the play" (177–83).

18. Calderwood, *To Be and Not To Be*, 144–48. But the linguistic model of action, with its fundamentally spatial orientation based on vertical and horizontal axes, is at odds with a phenomenological perception of time as always in the middle. For time, indeed, the wages of syntax is death.

19   See Avi Erlich, *Hamlet's Absent Father* (Princeton: Princeton University Press, 1977). Erlich maintains that the death of the father is perceived as weakness, and that Hamlet subsequently needs to prove his father's strength. See Richard Flatter, *Hamlet's Father* (London: Heinemann, 1947). In an unusual study of the ghost as an active character in the play, Flatter sees the ghost disappearing after the closet scene because Hamlet and his father are reconciled.

20. Merleau-Ponty, *Phenomenology of Perception*, 333.

21. Sypher views the change in Hamlet as an acceptance of punctiform time that opens the possibilities of the instant (*The Ethic of Time*, 65–89). See Maynard Mack, "The World of *Hamlet*." Mack, in his classic essay, sees the same change primarily as an acceptance of the existence of evil in the world.

22. Quinones focuses on the graveyard scene as a central illustration of Shakespeare's concern with a universal time scheme in the tragedies (*The Renaissance Discovery*, 387–98).

23. Barker, *The Tremulous Private Body*.

24. Booth, King Lear, 85. Booth examines both tragic theory and tragic structure as means of coping with "human nervousness at the fact of indefinition" (85). See in particular pp. 81–90.

25. See Elam, *Semiotics*, 143–44. Elam's semiotic approach accedes to the spatialization of time at least to the extent of allowing spatial deixis "priority over the temporal." His subsequent analysis of dramatic discourse is consequently more divergent from his theatrical theory than it need be.

Chapter 3. Put Your Discourse into Some Frame: *Hamlet* and the Uses of Wit

1.   Jones, *Hamlet and Oedipus*. Freud's suggestion was developed by Jones, first in 1910, then in a series of expanded versions culminating in the edition of 1949.

2.   Sigmund Freud, *Jokes and Their Relation to the Unconscious* (1905), trans. James Strachey (1960; New York: Norton, 1963).

3.   Geoffrey Bullough, ed., *Narrative and Dramatic Sources of Shakespeare*, 8 vols. (New York: Columbia University Press, 1973), vol. 7. See pp. 3–59 for the provenance of the Hamlet story; pp. 60–79 for the version by Saxo Grammaticus.

4.   Freud, *Jokes*, 159–80.

5.   Jacques Lacan, *Écrits: A Selection*, trans. Alan Sheridan (New York: Norton, 1977).

6.   Bergson, "Laughter," in *Comedy*, ed. Wylie Sypher (Garden City, N.Y.: Doubleday, 1956), 63.

7.   Lacan singles out the ability to "pretend to pretend" as uniquely human (*Écrits*, 305). Freud selects a joke in which telling the truth is perceived as lying to exemplify the skeptical joke, that which attacks the certainty of knowledge (*Jokes*, 115).

8.   Lacan, *Écrits*, 155.

9.   Charney, *Style in* Hamlet. Charney notes the unusual variety of Hamlet's styles: self-conscious (chiefly parodic), passionate (chiefly in soliloquy), witty, and simple (258–313). As we examine the dynamics of the play we will tend to find the witty displaced by the self-conscious (and, although it is not my focus here, the passionate by the simple) when we reach Act V.

10. Wolfgang Iser, "The Art of Failure: The Stifled Laugh in Beckett's Theater," *Bucknell Review* 26, no. 1 (1981): 139–89. Iser, in an examination of stifled laughter in Beckett cites a similar dramatic strategy. In *Godot*, "the overall plotline seems to be the background against which the comic paradigms lose their humor" (154).

11. Jean Alter, "From Text to Performance: Semiotics of Theatrality," *Poetics Today* 2, no. 3 (1981): 130, 133–34.

12. Susan Snyder, *The Comic Matrix of Shakespeare's Tragedies* (Princeton: Princeton University Press, 1979). Snyder views *Hamlet* as a "tragedy of multiplicity" in which the protagonist seeks a sense of pattern (91–136). I would merely add that before Hamlet can find meaning he must dissolve meaning. See Booth, "On the Value of *Hamlet*," 137–76. Booth has observed the sense of intellectual athleticism on the part of the audience as it experiences the movement of Hamlet's mind as well as the sense that it "gets information or sees action it once wanted only after a new interest has superseded the old" (143).

13. See Lionel Abel, *Metatheatre: A New View of Dramatic Form* (New York: Hill and Wang, 1963). Among the formulations of the play which deal with Hamlet's refusal to accept the rhetorical or dramatic frameworks of others, Abel sees Hamlet as playwright demanding his own script (40–58). See Elam, *Semiotics*; Elam examines Hamlet's disruption of speech acts (175). Susan Snyder describes the patterns of deflection in the play's structure as "akin to the evitability of comedy" (*The Comic Matrix*, 121). See Alvin B. Kernan, *The Playwright as Magician; Shakespeare's Image*

of the Poet in the English Public Theater (New Haven: Yale University Press, 1979). Kernan sees in the succession of internal plays that constitute the "latent theater" in *Hamlet* the implication that "the truth of all the plays is ambiguous and provisional" (111).

14. Bergson, "Laughter," 94.
15. The eiron's multiple awareness is central to Susan Snyder's conception of Hamlet. I argue his consciousness of comedy rather than his predominance within a comic structure.
16. Bergson, "Laughter," 67.
17. See Calderwood, *To Be and Not To Be*. Calderwood views the extensive negation in *Hamlet* as logocidal (53–58). The logocidal impulse is ultimately related to "the disintegration of proper differences" (63). Hamlet's puns too are viewed as a form of negation: "Wordplay intrudes the eraser of negation between signifiers and signifieds" (80).
18. Elaine Showalter, "Representing Ophelia: Women, Madness and the Responsibilities of Feminist Criticism," in *Shakespeare and the Question of Theory*, ed. Patricia Parker and Geoffrey Hartman (London: Methuen, 1985), 77–94. Showalter argues that the discourse on Ophelia "changes independently of theories of the meaning of the play or the Prince, for it depends on attitudes towards women and madness" (92). Such a result is an extension of the way Ophelia is treated within the play.
19. See, for example, Barker, *The Tremulous Private Body*, 39–40.
20. I have been concerned with the rehabilitation of the name "king"; Calderwood focuses on this scene as the place where Hamlet distinguishes himself from his father as well as affirms his kinship, giving meaning to the name Hamlet (*To Be and Not To Be,* 34–41).
21. See Booth, King Lear. At this point the invitation to laughter is direct rather than equivocal. In terms Booth (1983) uses to compare comedy and tragedy, now the comic proposition "that there is a way things are and fools forget what it is" takes precedence over the tragic proposition "that there is a way things are and that fools assume it is knowable and known" (78).

Chapter 4. About, My Brains!: Hamlet's Soliloquies

1. Charney, "Asides, Soliloquies, and Offstage Speech in *Hamlet*: Implications for Staging," in *Shakespeare and the Sense of Performance*, ed. Marvin and Ruth Thompson (Newark: University of Delaware Press, 1989), 116–31.
2. Ralph Berry, "Hamlet and the Audience: The Dynamics of a Relationship," in *Shakespeare and the Sense of Performance*, ed. Marvin and Ruth Thompson (Newark: University of Delaware Press, 1989), 24–28.

3.   G. Blakemore Evans, ed., *The Riverside Shakespeare* (Boston: Houghton Mifflin, 1974), 1191.
4.   Jacques Derrida, *Of Grammatology*, trans. Gayatri Chakravorty Spivak (Baltimore: Johns Hopkins University Press, 1976), 6–26.
5.   Goldman, *Acting and Action in Shakespearean Tragedy* (Princeton: Princeton University Press, 1985).
6.   Calderwood, *To Be and Not To Be*, 156.
7.   Marvin Rosenberg, "Subtext in Shakespeare," in *Shakespeare and the Sense of Performance*, ed. Marvin and Ruth Thompson (Newark: University of Delaware Press, 1989), 79–90.
8.   See Erlich, *Hamlet's Absent Father*, 52–56. For Erlich, this disengagement is significant in coming to terms with the absent father.
9.   See Roland Mushat Frye, *The Renaissance* Hamlet: *Issues and Responses in 1600* (Princeton: Princeton University Press, 1984), 135. Frye sees this scene as taking the "mighty opposites" to the verge of role reversal for the Renaissance audience.
10. Calderwood, *To Be and Not To Be*, 79.
11. Erving Goffman, *Forms of Talk* (Philadelphia: University of Pennsylvania Press, 1981), 78–84.
12. John Barton, *Playing Shakespeare* (London: Methuen, 1984), 94.
13. Geoffrey H. Hartman, *Saving the Text: Literature/Derrida/Philosophy* (Baltimore: Johns Hopkins University Press, 1981), 133.
14. See Svetlana Alpers, *The Art of Describing: Dutch Art in the Seventeenth Century* (Chicago: University of Chicago Press, 1983), 26–71.

Chapter 5. Body, Actor, and Character in *Hamlet*

1.   For semiological approaches to theater, see Pavis, *Languages of the Stage*. See Alessandro Serpieri, et al., "Toward a Segmentation of the Dramatic Text," *Poetics Today* 2, no. 3 (1981): 163–200. Serpieri significantly links the dramatic text to conditions of performance (165). For an overview of theatrical perspectives on the dramatic text, see Elam, *Semiotics*.
2.   See Denis Diderot, "The Paradox of Acting," in *Actors on Acting*, ed. Toby Cole and Helen Krich Chinoy (New York: Crown, 1949), 162–70. In *The Paradox of Acting* (c. 1773), arguing against a theater of sensibility, Diderot claimed of the actor: "He must have in himself an unmoved and disinterested onlooker" (162).
3.   See David Leverentz, "The Woman in Hamlet: An Interpersonal View," in *Representing Shakespeare: New Psychoanalytic Essays*, ed. Murray M. Schwartz and Coppélia Kahn (Baltimore: Johns Hopkins University Press, 1980), 110–28. Leverentz sees "the woman in Hamlet" in his kinship with Ophelia and Gertrude as victims of paternal duplicities: "The manly identity is imposed, not grown into" (125). See Linda Bamber, *Comic*

Women, Tragic Men: A Study of Gender and Genre in Shakespeare (Stanford, Calif.: Stanford University Press, 1982), 71–90. Bamber sees Hamlet as having "negative sexuality," largely expressed in misogyny, until he has his desire with Rosencrantz and Guildenstern in an act of aggression "imagined as a rape."

4. See Alter, "From Text to Performance," 128.
5. Howard Felperin, *Shakespearean Representation: Mimesis and Modernity in Elizabethan Tragedy* (Princeton: Princeton University Press, 1977), 59.
6. A. D. Nuttall, *A New Mimesis: Shakespeare and the Representation of Reality* (London: Methuen, 1983), 49.
7. Felperin, *Shakespearean Representation,* 66.
8. Wladimir Krysinski, "Semiotic Modalities of the Body in Modern Theater," *Poetics Today* 2, no. 3 (1981): 141.
9. See Barker, *The Tremulous Private Body.* For Barker, however, *Hamlet* is a play which gestures toward an interiority that is historically premature because it precedes the Cartesian intervention (22–41).
10. Abel, *Metatheatre.* The net effect of the literature on metatheater and metadrama is to focus attention on the spectator's participation in the theatrical contract. For Abel, a character must "collaborate in his dramatization" to be considered self-conscious (58), but in Abel's somewhat mystical conception, death is the final playwright in *Hamlet.* Sidney Homan, on the other hand, finds Hamlet's theatrical perspective enervating in the face of reality (*When the Theater Turns to Itself,* 152–76). For Calderwood, Hamlet disillusions us about illusion only to create the duck-rabbit of a theater that simultaneously deconstructs and constructs itself (*To Be and Not To Be*, 166–75). See Richard Hornby, *Drama, Metadrama, and Perception* (Lewisburg, Pa.: Bucknell University Press, 1986). Hornby sees an always self-referential drama/culture project at work (13–28). Elam concludes that theater's metatheatrical or metadramatic gestures are means of confirming the framework that makes possible the theatrical event (*Semiotics,* 90).
11. Serpieri, "Toward a Segmentation," 175.
12. Joseph Chaikin, *The Presence of the Actor* (New York: Atheneum, 1980), 20.
13. For an overview on speech acts in the theater, see Elam, *Semiotics,* 156–70; for deixis, 138–48.
14. Anne Ubersfeld, *Lire le théâtre* (Paris: Editions Sociales, 1977), 33.
15. Pavis, *Languages of the Stage,* 72–73.
16. Elam, *Semiotics,* 38.
17. Bert O. States, *Great Reckonings in Little Rooms: On the Phenomenology of Theater* (Berkeley: University of California Press, 1985), 136.
18 Chaikin, *The Presence of the Actor,* 69.
19. Berger, "Text Against Performance in Shakespeare," 78.
20. See Merleau-Ponty, *Phenomenology of Perception.*

21.   See Robert Weimann, "Mimesis in *Hamlet*," in *Shakespeare and the Question of Theory*, ed. Patricia Parker and Geoffrey Hartman (London: Methuen, 1985), 275–91; Alvin B. Kernan, *The Playwright as Magician*. Weimann views the diversity of mimetic theories as a reflection of a tension between a humanist theory of representation and histrionic practice (281). Kernan suggests that instrumental theories of theater are rendered fundamentally unstable in *Hamlet* by the evolving world-as-play mysticism which culminates in *The Tempest* (85–111).

22.   Antonin Artaud, *The Theater and Its Double*, trans. Mary Caroline Richards (New York: Grove, 1958), 15–32.

23.   Merleau-Ponty, *Phenomenology of Perception*, 183.

24.   See David Bevington, *Action Is Eloquence: Shakespeare's Language of Gesture* (Cambridge: Harvard University Press, 1984). Bevington's study of the language of visual signs in Shakespeare's plays contrasts the potential inadequacies and duplicities of conventional visual signs with the desire for a world of neoplatonic correspondences. Hamlet's dumb show suggests how the use of the body as instrument problematizes the simple polarization of representation and misrepresentation (1–34, 67–98).

25.   The definition of theatrical frames has followed the terminology of Gregory Bateson and Erving Goffman. Crucial to the theatrical frame is that spectators and performers are distinguished (Elam, *Semiotics*, 87–92).

26.   See Goldman, *Acting and Action in Shakespearean Tragedy*. Alternatively, Goldman examines the term "action" in Aristotelian terms, viewing action as a bridge between the self and the world (6). In examining *Hamlet*, he is moved to introduce the expression "spectrum of action," moving Aristotle's discrete terminology toward a continuum (17–45). The approach is most concerned with the "To be or not to be" soliloquy, and regards the fencing scene as a "sublime trick" (27).

Chapter 6. Issues of Culture and Genre

1.   See Arthur C. Kirsch, *Jacobean Dramatic Perspectives* (Charlottesville: University Press of Virginia, 1972).

2.   See Helge Kökeritz, ed., *Mr. William Shakespeares Comedies, Histories, & Tragedies* (London, 1623; New Haven: Yale University Press, 1954).

3.   See Bamber, *Comic Women*, who explores the issue across the canon.

4.   Bowers, *Elizabethan Revenge Tragedy*.

5.   Francis Bacon, "Of Revenge," in *Essays* (1597, 1625; London: Oxford University Press, 1937), 18–19.

6.   F. L. Lucas, *Seneca and Elizabethan Tragedy* (1922; New York: Haskell House, 1966). Prosser, *Hamlet and Revenge*. See Bowers, *Elizabethan Revenge Tragedy*, 101–53.

7. Umberto Eco, *Semiotics and the Philosophy of Language* (Bloomington: Indiana University Press, 1986), 163.
8. E. D. Hirsch, Jr., *Validity in Interpretation* (New Haven: Yale University Press, 1967), 125.
9. Ibid., 86.
10. Eco, *Semiotics and the Philosophy of Language* (Bloomington: Indiana University Press, 1986), 163.
11. Ibid., 162.
12. Ibid., 158.
13. Umberto Eco, *A Theory of Semiotics* (Bloomington: Indiana University Press, 1957), 138.
14. See Walter N. King, *Hamlet's Search for Meaning*, who explores Hamlet's relation to Christian Providence and acknowledges its inherent ambiguity.
15. Richard Schechner, "The End of Humanism," in *The End of Humanism: Writings on Performance* (New York: Performing Arts Journal Publications, 1982), 95–106.
16. Ernest and Henry Brennecke, eds. and trans., *Der Bestrafte Brudermord*, in *Shakespeare in Germany 1590–1700* (Chicago: University of Chicago Press, 1964), 253–90.
17. E. D. Hirsch, Jr., uses the neutral term "traits" (*Validity in Interpretation*, 50). See Alastair Fowler, *Kinds of Literature: An Introduction to the Theory of Genres and Modes* (Cambridge: Harvard University Press, 1982). Fowler discusses generic "signals" (88–105).
18. Cyril Tourneur, *The Atheist's Tragedy*, ed. Brian Morris and Roma Gill (London: Ernest Benn, 1976).
19. David Bevington, *Action Is Eloquence*, 178–79.
20. Francis Fergusson, *The Idea of a Theater* (Princeton: Princeton University Press, 1949), 114.
21. Geoffrey Bullough, ed., *Narrative and Dramatic Sources*, vol. 7. See books 3-4 of *Historiae Danicae* by Saxo Grammaticus (60–79).
22. Barker, *The Tremulous Private Body*.
23. Maria Corti, *An Introduction to Literary Semiotics*, trans. Margherita Bogat and Allen Mandelbaum (Bloomington: Indiana University Press, 1978), 115–43. In her examination of genre as program, Corti notes that from a distance we are likely to find that "the offense to the norm is more enjoyable than obsequiousness to it" (132).
24. Robert Weimann, "Mimesis in *Hamlet*," 278. See also Robert Weimann, *Shakespeare and the Popular Tradition in the Theater*, ed. Robert Schwartz (Baltimore: Johns Hopkins University Press, 1978), 126–33. Weimann establishes primitive precedents for Hamlet's antic disposition in English folk plays.
25. See Bowers, *Elizabethan Revenge Tragedy*, 130–32.
26. Gilbert Murray, *Hamlet and Orestes: A Study in Traditional Types* (New York: Oxford University Press, 1914).

27. See Rosalie L. Colie, *The Resources of Kind: Genre-Theory in the Renaissance*, ed. Barbara K. Lewalski (Berkeley: University of California Press, 1973), 103–28. Colie examines the conflict of commitments involved in mixing genres.

Works Cited

Abel, Lionel. *Metatheatre: A New View of Dramatic Form*. New York: Hill and Wang, 1963.

Alpers, Svetlana. *The Art of Describing: Dutch Art in the Seventeenth Century*. Chicago: University of Chicago Press, 1983.

Alter, Jean. "From Text to Performance: Semiotics of Theatrality." *Poetics Today* 2, no. 3 (1981): 113–39.

Aristotle. *The Poetics*. Translated by S. H. Butcher. London: Macmillan, 1911.

Arnheim, Rudolf. *The Power of the Center: A Study of Composition in the Visual Arts*. Rev. ed. Berkeley: University of California Press, 1982.

Artaud, Antonin. *The Theater and Its Double*. Translated by Mary Caroline Richards. New York: Grove Press, 1958.

Bacon, Francis. "Of Revenge." In *Essays* (1597, 1625). London: Oxford University Press, 1937.

Bamber, Linda. *Comic Women, Tragic Men: A Study of Gender and Genre in Shakespeare*. Stanford, Calif.: Stanford University Press, 1982.

Barker, Francis. *The Tremulous Private Body: Essays on Subjection*. London: Methuen, 1984.

Barton, John. *Playing Shakespeare*. London: Methuen, 1984.

Beckerman, Bernard. *Dynamics of Drama: Theory and Method of Analysis* (1970). New York: Drama Book Specialists, 1979.

Berger, Harry, Jr. "Text Against Performance in Shakespeare: The Example of *MacBeth*." *Genre* 7 (1982): 49–79.

Bergson, Henri. "Laughter." In *Comedy*, edited by Wylie Sypher. Garden City, N.Y.: Doubleday, 1956.

———. *Time and Free Will*. Translated by F. L. Pogson. 4th ed. New York: Macmillan, 1921.

Berry, Ralph. "Hamlet and the Audience: The Dynamics of a Relation-
    ship." In *Shakespeare and the Sense of Performance,* edited by Marvin
    and Ruth Thompson. Newark: University of Delaware Press, 1989.
Bevington, David. *Action Is Eloquence: Shakespeare's Language of
    Gesture.* Cambridge: Harvard University Press, 1984.
Blau, Herbert. *Blooded Thought: Occasions of Theatre.* New York:
    Performing Arts Journal, 1982.
Booth, Stephen. King Lear, Macbeth, *Indefinition and Tragedy.* New
    Haven: Yale University Press, 1983.
————. "On the Value of *Hamlet.*" In *Reinterpretations of Elizabethan
    Drama: Selected Papers From the English Institute*, edited by Norman
    Rabkin. New York: Columbia University Press, 1969.
Bowers, Fredson. *Elizabethan Revenge Tragedy.* Princeton: Princeton
    University Press, 1940.
Brennecke, Ernest, and Henry Brennecke, eds. and trans. *Der Bestrafte
    Brudermord.* In *Shakespeare in Germany 1590-1700.* Chicago:
    University of Chicago Press, 1964.
Brook, Peter. *The Empty Space.* New York: Atheneum, 1978.
Bullough, Geoffrey, ed. *Narrative and Dramatic Sources of Shakespeare.*
    8 vols. New York: Columbia University Press, 1973.
Calderwood, James L. *To Be and Not To Be: Negation and Metadrama
    in* Hamlet. New York: Columbia University Press, 1983.
Chaikin, Joseph. *The Presence of the Actor.* New York: Atheneum, 1980.
Charney, Maurice. "Asides, Soliloquies, and Offstage Speech in *Hamlet*:
    Implications for Staging." In *Shakespeare and the Sense of
    Performance*, edited by Marvin and Ruth Thompson. Newark:
    University of Delaware Press, 1989.
————. *Style in* Hamlet. Princeton: Princeton University Press, 1969.
Colie, Rosalie L. *The Resources of Kind: Genre Theory in the
    Renaissance.* Edited by Barbara Lewalski. Berkeley: University of
    California Press, 1973.
Corti, Maria. *An Introduction to Literary Semiotics.* Translated by
    Margherita Bogat and Allen Mandelbaum. Bloomington: Indiana
    University Press, 1978.
Derrida, Jacques. *Of Grammatology.* Translated by Gayatri Chakravorty
    Spivak. Baltimore: Johns Hopkins University Press, 1976.
Dessen, Alan C. *Elizabethan Drama and the Viewer's Eye.* Chapel Hill:
    University of North Carolina Press, 1977.

Diderot, Denis. "The Paradox of Acting." In *Actors on Acting*, edited by Toby Cole and Helen Krich Chinoy. New York: Crown, 1949.

Eco, Umberto. *Semiotics and the Philosophy of Language*. Bloomington: Indiana University Press, 1986.

———. *A Theory of Semiotics*. Bloomington: Indiana University Press, 1957.

Elam, Keir. *The Semiotics of Theatre and Drama*. London: Methuen, 1980.

Erikson, Erik H. *Identity: Youth and Crisis*. New York: Norton 1968.

Erlich, Avi. *Hamlet's Absent Father*. Princeton: Princeton University Press, 1977.

Evans, G. Blakemore, ed. *The Riverside Shakespeare*. Boston: Houghton Mifflin, 1974.

Felperin, Howard. *Shakespearean Representation: Mimesis and Modernity in Elizabethan Tragedy*. Princeton: Princeton University Press, 1977.

Fergusson, Francis. *The Idea of a Theater*. Princeton: Princeton University Press, 1949.

Flatter, Richard. *Hamlet's Father*. London: Heinemann: 1947.

Fowler, Alastair. *Kinds of Literature: An Introduction to the Theory of Genres and Modes*. Cambridge: Harvard University Press, 1982.

Freud, Sigmund. *Jokes and Their Relation to the Unconscious*. (1905). Translated by James Strachey. 1960. New York: Norton, 1963.

Frye, Roland Mushat. *The Renaissance* Hamlet: *Issues and Responses in 1600*. Princeton: Princeton University Press, 1984.

Garber, Marjorie. *Coming of Age in Shakespeare*. New York: Methuen, 1981.

Goffman, Erving. *Forms of Talk*. Philadelphia: University of Pennsylvania Press, 1981.

Goldman, Michael. *Acting and Action in Shakespearean Tragedy*. Princeton: Princeton University Press, 1985.

———. *The Actor's Freedom: Toward a Theory of Drama*. New York: Viking, 1975.

Granville-Barker, Harley. *Prefaces to Shakespeare*. Vol. 1. Princeton: Princeton University Press, 1946.

Grebanier, Bernard. *The Heart of* Hamlet. New York: Crowell, 1960.

Greenblatt, Stephen. *Shakespearean Negotiations: The Circulation of Social Energy in Renaissance England*. Berkeley: University of California Press, 1988.

Hapgood, Robert. "*Hamlet* Nearly Absurd: The Dramaturgy of Delay." *Tulane Drama Review* 9 (1965): 132–45.

Hartman, Geoffrey H. *Saving the Text: Literature/Derrida/Philosophy*. Baltimore: Johns Hopkins University Press, 1981.

Hirsch, E.D., Jr. *Validity in Interpretation*. New Haven: Yale University Press, 1967.

Homan, Sidney. *Shakespeare's Theater of Presence: Language, Spectacle, and the Audience*. Lewisburg, Pa.: Bucknell University Press, 1989.

———. *When the Theater Turns to Itself: The Aesthetic Metaphor in Shakespeare*. Lewisburg, Pa.: Bucknell University Press, 1986.

Hornby, Richard. *Drama, Metadrama, and Perception*. Lewisburg, Pa.: Bucknell University Press, 1986.

Iser, Wolfgang. "The Art of Failure: The Stifled Laugh in Beckett's Theater." *Bucknell Review* 26, no. 1 (1981): 139–89.

Jones, Ernest. *Hamlet and Oedipus* (1949). New York: Norton, 1976.

Kastan, David Scott. *Shakespeare and the Shapes of Time*. Hanover, N.H.: University Press of New England, 1982.

Kernan, Alvin B. *The Playwright as Magician: Shakespeare's Image of the Poet in the English Public Theater*. New Haven: Yale University Press, 1979.

King, Walter N. *Hamlet's Search for Meaning*. Athens: University of Georgia Press, 1982.

Kirsch, Arthur C. *Jacobean Dramatic Perspectives*. Charlottesville: University Press of Virginia, 1972.

Kökeritz, Helge, ed. *Mr. William Shakespeares Comedies, Histories, & Tragedies*. London, 1623; New Haven: Yale University Press, 1954.

Koyré, Alexandre. *From the Closed World to the Infinite Universe*. Baltimore: Johns Hopkins University Press, 1957.

Krysinski, Wladimir. "Semiotic Modalities of the Body in Modern Theater." *Poetics Today* 2, no. 3 (1981): 141-61.

Lacan, Jacques. *Écrits: A Selection*. Translated by Alan Sheridan. New York: Norton, 1977.

Langer, Susanne K. *Feeling and Form*. New York: Charles Scribner's Sons, 1953.

Leverentz, David. "The Woman in Hamlet: An Interpersonal View." In *Representing Shakespeare: New Psychoanalytic Essays*, edited by Murray M. Schwartz and Coppélia Kahn. Baltimore: Johns Hopkins University Press, 1980.

Lucas, F. L. *Seneca and Elizabethan Tragedy*. 1922. New York: Haskell House, 1966.

Mack, Maynard. "The World of *Hamlet*." *The Yale Review* 41 (1952): 502–23.

Merleau-Ponty, M. *Phenomenology of Perception*. Translated by Colin Smith. New York: Humanities University Press, 1962.

Murray, Gilbert. *Hamlet and Orestes: A Study in Traditional Types*. New York: Oxford University Press, 1914.

Nardo, Anna K. "Hamlet, 'A Man to Double Business Bound.'" *Shakespeare Quarterly* 34 (1983): 181–89.

Nuttall, A.D. *A New Mimesis: Shakespeare and the Representation of Reality*. London: Methuen, 1983.

Ong, Walter, S.J. *Ramus, Method, and the Decay of Dialogue*. Cambridge: Harvard University Press, 1958.

Pavis, Patrice. *Languages of the Stage: Essays in the Semiology of Theatre*. New York: Performing Arts Journal Publications, 1982.

Prosser, Eleanor. Hamlet *and Revenge*. Stanford, Calif.: Stanford University Press, 1967.

Quinones, Ricardo J. *The Renaissance Discovery of Time*. Cambridge: Harvard University Press, 1972.

Rabkin, Norman. *Shakespeare and the Common Understanding*. Chicago: University of Chicago Press, 1967.

Rosenberg, Marvin. *The Masks of Hamlet*. Newark: University of Delaware Press, 1992.

———. "Subtext in Shakespeare." In *Shakespeare and the Sense of Performance*, edited by Marvin and Ruth Thompson. Newark: University of Delaware Press, 1989.

Schechner, Richard. *The End of Humanism: Writings on Performance*. New York: Performing Arts Journal Publications, 1982.

Serpieri, Alessandro, et al. "Toward a Segmentation of the Dramatic Text." *Poetics Today* 2, no. 3 (1982): 163-200.

Shakespeare, William. *A New Variorum Edition of Shakespeare: Hamlet*. 4th ed. 3 vols. Edited by H. H. Furness. Philadelphia: Lippencott, 1877.

Showalter, Elaine. "Representing Ophelia: Women, Madness and the Responsibilities of Feminist Criticism." In *Shakespeare and the Question of Theory*, edited by Patricia Parker and Geoffrey Hartman. London: Methuen, 1985.

Snyder, Susan. *The Comic Matrix of Shakespeare's Tragedies*. Princeton: Princeton University Press, 1979.

Spurgeon, Caroline F.E. *Shakespeare's Imagery and What It Tells Us*. Cambridge: Cambridge University Press, 1935.

States, Bert O. *Great Reckonings in Little Rooms: On the Phenomenology of Theater*. Berkeley: University of California Press, 1985.

Styan, John L. "Stage Space and the Shakespeare Experience." In *Shakespeare and the Sense of Performance*. Edited by Marvin and Ruth Thompson. Newark: University of Delaware Press, 1989.

————. *The Shakespeare Revolution*. Cambridge: Cambridge University Press, 1977.

Sypher, Wylie. *The Ethic of Time: Structures of Experience in Shakespeare*. New York: Seabury, 1976.

Tourneur, Cyril. *The Atheist's Tragedy*. Edited by Brian Morris and Roma Gill. London: Ernest Benn, 1976.

Ubersfeld, Anne. *Lire le théâtre*. Paris: Editions Sociales, 1977.

Webster, John. *The White Devil*. Vol. 1 of *Jacobean Drama: An Anthology*, edited by Richard C. Harrier. 1963. New York: Norton, 1968.

Weimann, Robert. "Mimesis in *Hamlet*." In *Shakespeare and the Question of Theory*, edited by Patricia Parker and Geoffrey Hartman. London: Methuen, 1985.

————. *Shakespeare and the Popular Tradition in the Theater*. Edited by Robert Schwartz. Baltimore: Johns Hopkins University Press, 1978.

Wilson, J. Dover. *What Happens in Hamlet*. 3rd ed. Cambridge: Cambridge University Press, 1951.

Index

Abel, Lionel, 117, 156 n.13, 159 n.10
Aeschylus, 70; *Oresteia*, 28, 147, 150;
    academic versions of the Orestes saga,
    133
Alter, Jean, 76, 113–14
Amleth, 72, 74, 141, 144–45, 148–49
Aristotle, 49, 112, 142, 144, 160 n.26
Arnheim, Rudolf, 42
Artaud, Antonin, 121–22

Bacon, Francis, 133
Bamber, Linda, 158–59 n.3, 160 n.3
Barker, Francis, 44, 64, 143
Barton, John, 107
Bateson, Gregory, 154 n.16, 160 n.25
Beaumont and Fletcher: *The Maid's
    Tragedy*, 134
Beckerman, Bernard, 154 n.8
Beckett, Samuel: *Waiting for Godot*, 47,
    156 n.10
Berger, Harry Jr., 120, 152 n.3
Bergson, Henri, 48, 73, 78, 153 n.4
Berry, Ralph, 92
Bestrafte Brudermord, Der, 97, 137–38
Bevington, David, 140
Blau, Herbert, 50
Booth, Stephen, 50, 65, 155 n.24, 156 n.12,
    157 n.21
Bowers, Fredson, 133, 136, 152 n.7
Brook, Peter, 151 n.1
Bruno, Giordano, 39

Calderwood, James L., 56–57, 99, 106,
    152 n.5, 155 n.18, 157 n.17, 159 n.10
Chaikin, Joseph, 118–19, 121
Chapman, George, 145

Charney, Maurice, 92, 152–53 n.12,
    154 n.8, 156 n.9
Chekhov, Anton: *The Cherry Orchard*, 29
Chettle, Henry: *Hoffman*, 139
Colie, Rosalie L., 162 n.27
Corti, Maria, 161 n.22

Day-Lewis, Daniel, 19
Derrida, Jacques, 98
Dessen, Alan C., 153 n.18
Diderot, Denis, 112, 158 n.2

Eco, Umberto, 135–36
Elam, Keir, 119, 154 n.9, 155 n.25,
    156 n.13, 160 n.25
Eliot, T. S., 143
Erikson, Erik H., 154 n.16
Erlich, Avi, 155 n.19, 158 n.8
Euripedes, 70; *Medea*, 28
Existentialism, 17, 135, 152 n.6

Felperin, Howard, 115
Fergusson, Francis, 141
Film, 13, 20–21, 106, 118, 131–32, 144.
    See also Olivier; Zeffirelli
Flatter, Richard, 155 n.19
Fowler, Alastair, 161 n.17
French symbolists, 135
Freud, Sigmund, 13, 69–73, 81, 95,
    156 n.7; "talking cure," 143
Freudian and psychological criticism, 17,
    19, 44, 50, 53, 69, 115, 135, 154–
    55 n.16. *See also* Lacan
Frye, Roland Mushat, 158 n.9

Garber, Marjorie, 154–55 n.16

169